. . . a resource of student workshops, activities, and strategies to accompany

WRITE SOURCE 2000

WRITE SOURCE

GREAT SOURCE EDUCATION GROUP
a Houghton Mifflin Company
Wilmington, Massachusetts

A FEW WORDS ABOUT SOURCEBOOK 8000

■ **Below are some of the people who developed your SourceBook.**

Authors: Pat Sebranek
Dave Kemper
Randall VanderMey

Contributing Teachers:
Pat Andrews
Laura Bachman
Gina Camodeca
Carol Elsholz
Candice Fortmann
Tom Gilding
Mary Gregory
Janis Hartley
Phyllis Jaeger
Bev Jessen
Bonnie Knoblauch
Dale Ann Morgan
Peg Rifken
V. Kelly Saaf
Pat Santilli
Cynthia Stock
Betsy Watson

Editor: Lois Krenzke
Graphics: Sherry Gordon
Illustrator: Chris Krenzke

Before you begin . . .

it is important for you to know that your *SourceBook 8000* must be used with the *Write Source 2000* handbook. The handbook provides guidelines, examples, and models; the SourceBook provides many opportunities to put that information into practice. It's also important for you to know how all of the activities in the SourceBook are organized.

Part I contains seven core writing units that address many of the important forms of writing covered in the handbook, including autobiographical and biographical writing, paragraphs, essays, and stories.

Part II contains many different workshop activities that will help you at all stages of the writing process, from prewriting to proofreading.

Part III contains language workshops that will help you better understand how words work, and learning workshops that will help you become a better thinker, study-reader, speaker, and listener.

Part IV, way in the back of the book, features a series of minilessons that relate to all of the different areas of writing, language, and learning covered in your handbook.

What makes "shopping" in your SourceBook so worthwhile is that the activities come in so many different shapes and sizes; there is something to please everybody. All you and your teacher have to do is decide what units and workshops best meet your needs. We're sure that all of your shopping experiences in this SourceBook will help you improve as a writer and as a learner.

TABLE OF CONTENTS

What You'll Find Inside

Part I: Core Writing Units

Part II: Writing Workshops

Part III: Language and Learning Workshops

Part IV: Writing and Learning Minilessons

PART I
Core Writing Units

CORE WRITING UNITS

Writing from Start to Finish

The **Core Writing Units** provide you with a series of seven extended writing activities addressing many of the basic types of writing covered in the *Write Source 2000* student handbook: autobiographical writing, paragraphs, essays, and stories. As you complete your work in these units, you will be gaining valuable experience with the types of writing tasks you are often asked to carry out in your classes, as well as in most writing assessment tests. You will also be practicing the very skills that are at the "core" of the writing process, from selecting subjects to correcting final drafts.

It's important to know that everything you need to complete your work is included, from step-by-step guidelines to student models. In addition, each page within these units is self-contained, providing you with clearly identifiable starting and stopping points for your work. This will make it easy for you to stay on task from one day to the next. Upon completion of each unit, you will have produced at least one important piece of writing.

User's Checklist

Check your progress as you work on these **Core Writing Units.**

☐ **Writing the Phase Autobiography**
And what about you?

☐ **Building Paragraphs**
Expository Writing

☐ **Building Essays**
Multiparagraph Writing

☐ **Writing the Phase Biography**
What was it really like?

☐ **Writing a Survival Story**
Put to the Test

☐ **Cause and Effect Writing**
Here Today, Gone Tomorrow

☐ **Writing to Define**
de•fine: to determine or identify the meaning of . . .

FOLLOW-UP • Does your teacher expect you to turn in a writing portfolio at the end of the grading period? If so, reserve some space in it for the writing you complete in these units.

WRITING THE PHASE AUTOBIOGRAPHY

And what about you?

START-UP • In the opening remarks to "Writing Phase Autobiographies" in the handbook, we are told that "at different points in our lives, we all live through 'phases' . . . extended periods of time that affect us, change us, make us better or make us different. They help make us who we are . . ."

In this unit, you will have an opportunity to explore different phases or extended periods of time in your life. You will also select one specific period of time to write about in a **phase autobiography**. Your work in this unit will help you tap into your best resource of information—yourself—when it comes to writing. And it will help you come to understand more fully who you really are and where you have been.

HANDBOOK HELPER   You will be asked to read different parts of "Writing Phase Autobiographies" throughout this unit. Refer to "Phase autobiography" in the index for this chapter.

FREE-WRITE: Take a minute to study the following graphic; then write freely for 8-10 minutes on your own paper, focusing your thoughts (at least at the start of your writing) on one specific set of "wheels" in your past.

Wheels

FOLLOW-UP • Review your free writing to see what thoughts and feelings you uncovered. If your writing focused primarily on one set of wheels (perhaps your very first two-wheeler), you have explored a phase in your life. (Share the results of your work.)

■ Reading and Writing About Different Phases

READ: To find out what a phase autobiography looks and sounds like, read "Fashionation" in the handbook. (It is the first model in the "Writing Phase Autobiographies" chapter.) Note how the writer introduces her topic and how she develops her topic with specific examples and details.

REACT: Use the following checklist to help you respond to this model. (Share these responses with a classmate.)

_____ What do you like best about this writing? Was there, for example, a section you found particularly funny or a passage containing effective details? (List at least two things.)

_____ Are there any questions or concerns you have about the writing? For example, were any parts unclear? (Try to list at least one question or concern.)

_____ Does this writing call to mind any make-believe phases in your own life? (Try to identify at least one.)

FREE-WRITE: Write freely for 8-10 minutes, focusing your thoughts and feelings on the following writing prompt: "All good things must come to an end." (What good things have come to an end in your life? Perhaps a period of make-believe or a special friendship or a favorite year in school. Each one of these ideas could be considered a phase in your life.)

■ Reacting to and Exploring Another Phase

READ: To see how another phase autobiography was written, read "Mending a Wrong" by professional writer M. E. Kerr. Also note the introduction, side notes, and final thoughts in the model. (Again, you will find this model in "Writing Phase Autobiographies" in the handbook.)

REACT: Use the following checklist to help you respond to this model. (Share your responses with a classmate.)

_____ What do you like best about this model? (List one or two things.)

_____ What purpose seems to tie this model together? (Is the author trying to be funny and cute? Or is she trying to be serious and revealing? Or . . . ?)

_____ In what ways is this model different from "Fashionation"? (List at least two differences.)

_____ Does this model call to mind any phases in your life, any wrongs you would like to mend?

TALK ABOUT IT: Have a conversation with a friend about a related set of experiences from your past. Maybe you and your friend treated someone unfairly for a period of time. Maybe you were subjected to such treatment yourself. Then again, you might want to talk about something more upbeat and positive, like the summer you and your friend played T-ball together. Keep your conversation going as long as you can. Here's how it might start:

Me: Hey, Lee, you remember (a person's name) in fourth grade?

Lee: Yeah, what about him?

Me: He really juiced things up, didn't he? Remember when . . .

■ **Writing About One Incident**

High Points and Low Points

START-UP • At one time or another you might have experienced true elation. Elation is gold-plated happiness, happiness with a cherry on top, happiness that makes you sing and celebrate. (Maybe you won a contest or a game, earned an award or a reward, gained someone's respect, heard some great news, or so on.)

Or you may have experienced a great sadness, a sadness that really clouded over your whole life. (Maybe you had to move or lost a grandparent or a friend.)

WRITE: Think of a time when you experienced great happiness or sadness and write about it in a brief autobiographical sketch. Use the frame below to get you started. (Share your results—unless your writing is too personal.)

I felt like singing and celebrating (hiding my face in a pillow) when _____

_____ .

This experience has to be one of the highlights (low points) of my life. Let me tell you how

it all came about. _____

_____

_____

_____

_____

_____

_____

_____

_____ .

AFTER•THOUGHT This could be the starting point for a phase autobiography if you consider what happened before or after this experience, or if you had other experiences like this one.

■ Planning and Writing a Phase Autobiography

SELECTING: Think of an extended period of time in your life that you would like to write about in a phase autobiography. Your work in the previous activities in this unit should have generated possible subjects for this paper. If you need to conduct a subject search, try free writing or listing for ideas. Focus on a certain period of time like your earliest neighborhood memories.

COLLECTING & CONNECTING: Collect your thoughts about your subject in a freely written first draft. (Use the space below to get started on your first draft.)

(If you explored your subject in some detail in an earlier free writing, you already have, in effect, completed a first draft. If that is the case, try something different in this writing. You might, for example, re-create a typical conversation from this time or describe the main setting. Experiments like these add life to writing.)

_____

_____

_____

_____

_____

_____

_____

_____

_____

AFTER•THOUGHT Think of your first draft as the ground breaking, the all-important first step in the development of your writing. It's valuable and important to explore and experiment with your subject from a number of different angles.

■ Reviewing and Revising Your Writing

START-UP • As you review your first draft, decide what you like best about it as well as what seems to be missing or needs to be changed. Remember that you can't mention everything about your phase. Instead, you should try to focus on a few incidents that give readers a sense of the whole. (Do all of your revising and editing on your own paper.)

Helpful Hint: Establishing a purpose for your writing helps you tie everything together. Do you want to *entertain* your readers (as in the model "Fashionation"), cause them to *reevaluate* their own actions (as in "Mending a Wrong"), or . . . ?

EVALUATE: The following checklist will help you review and revise your phase autobiography. (Use this same checklist to evaluate your classmates' work.)

_____ **Organization:** Is the writing clearly organized around a particular phase or period of time?

_____ **Detail:** Are enough details included to make the subject come alive? (Consider the use of dialogue, sensory details, etc.)

_____ **Style:** Does the writing read smoothly from start to finish? And does the writing seem purposeful? That is, does it entertain, inform, surprise, or . . . ?

_____ **Mechanics:** Has proper attention been given to neatness and accuracy?

Additional Comments: (when reviewing a classmate's work)

_____ What do you like best about this phase autobiography? (List two things.)

_____ What changes would you recommend? (List at least one thing.)

HANDBOOK HELPER If you want to give your writing a special twist, look in the handbook for ideas. Refer specifically to "Shaping Your Writing for Your Readers" in the "Writing Phase Autobiographies" chapter.

BUILDING PARAGRAPHS

Expository Writing

WRITE: Complete a *topic sentence* for each of the general subjects listed below. Each topic sentence should include a *specific subject* and a *feeling* or an *attitude* associated with it. The first one is done for you. (Refer to "Paragraph, Basic parts" in the handbook index for a formula for writing topic sentences.)

(TV Show) *I am absolutely wild about* <u>Star Trek: The Next Generation.</u>

> *Formula:* A specific subject (*Star Trek*) + a specific feeling (*I am absolutely wild about*) = a good topic sentence.

(Book)

(Gym Class)

(Shoes)

(Food)

(Hair)

LIST: Make a list of details supporting one of the topic sentences from above. (List as many details as you feel are necessary.)

Write your topic sentence here: _____

_____

Detail 1:

Detail 2:

Detail 3:

Detail 4:

Detail 5:

FOLLOW-UP • On your own paper, write a paragraph using your topic sentence and the details you listed. The details should clearly support the topic sentence. Add a *closing* or *clincher sentence* after all of the details have been included.

■ Shaping Expository Paragraphs

Making "Arrangements"

START-UP • Suppose you were asked to write about your typical morning routine. No problem, right? It would simply be a matter of describing what you do first, second, third, and so on. Your response would be almost automatic. But suppose you were asked to answer one of the following questions in your writing:

- Which books (movies) rank as your four all-time favorites?
- What would your dream pizza look like?
- What does "respect" ("responsibility," "progress") mean to you?
- How much effort do you put into your schoolwork?
- Which athletes do you admire?

Now your writing task would be a little more difficult. And why? There's nothing automatic about an **expository** (explanatory) piece of writing. To explain something in an effective manner takes time, effort, and thought. You have to gather your details and then figure out the best way to arrange or organize them. (Refer to "Methods of arrangement" in the handbook index for more information on organizing ideas.)

WRITE: Answer one of the questions from above in an *expository paragraph*. Make sure to arrange your ideas and details in an effective way. (Use the space below for your finished copy.)

EXPOSITORY PARAGRAPH

_____

_____

_____

_____

_____

_____

_____

_____

FOLLOW-UP • Share your finished product with a classmate. During your sharing session, discuss how you selected and arranged the details in your writing.

■ Illustrating a Topic

There's a spider in my soup!

START-UP • All of us would lose our appetites at the sight of a spider skinny-dipping in our soup. An *arachniphobic* would lose her or his appetite . . . and then some. An arachniphobic (in case you didn't know) has a deep fear of spiders. If given a chance, someone with this fear would have many stories to tell about close encounters with these little creatures.

WRITE: **What about you? What fears or phobias do you have? Write about one of them in a paragraph. In your topic sentence, identify the subject of your fear. In the body of your paragraph, re-create a personal experience that clearly and effectively illustrates this subject. (Use the space below for your finished copy.)**

Note: What should you do if you're not afraid of anything? Pretend that you are and create a fearful experience.

ILLUSTRATING PARAGRAPH

_____

_____

_____

_____

_____

_____

_____

_____

_____

_____

_____

FOLLOW-UP • Divide into small groups of three or four students and share your work. Or better yet, have a sharing session with your entire class.

■ The Patterns in Paragraphs

It's just one thing after another.

START-UP • Generally, writers create meaning in their paragraphs by stating important ideas and supporting them with different levels of details. (This is how you write paragraphs.) There are, however, other ways in which writers create meaning in paragraphs. Read on and learn about one of these ways.

Example Paragraph

WRITE: Carefully read the example paragraph that follows. (Pay special attention to the beginning of each sentence.)

> Schools are asked to do far too many things. They are asked to provide meals for their students. They are asked to provide counseling for those students who need advice and guidance. They are asked to provide health care for those individuals who require medical attention. They are asked to provide a wide variety of programs to meet the special needs of students. They are asked to provide extracurricular activities. And, in addition to all of this, schools are asked to provide quality instruction for all.

Discussion: As you probably noted, almost every sentence in this paragraph begins with "Schools are asked . . ." or "They are asked . . . ." In addition, each sentence in the body of the paragraph expresses a single important idea. There are no follow-up details. In essence, this paragraph consists of a *list* of related and equally important ideas. It results in a powerful and effective piece of writing.

List 'n' Write

WRITE: On your own paper, write a "list" paragraph, using the example above as your guide. Make sure the sentences in your paragraph start in the same way and say something of equal importance. (The open-ended sentences that follow provide possible starting points for your paragraph.)

- Students really care about . . .
- Music is . . .
- We need to clean up . . .
- Money is . . .
- Grandparents are . . .
- Sports are . . .
- (A topic of your own choosing)

FOLLOW-UP • Share your list paragraph with a classmate. Those paragraphs that really "work" should be shared orally with the entire class.

■ **Summary Paragraphs**

Writing leads to learning.

START-UP • How's a poor ol' student like you ever going to make sense of all the learning material that comes your way? It's a challenge—no doubt about it. To lighten your learning load, we offer the following advice: Use writing as your personal learning tool. Writing slows your thinking process down, so to speak, and allows you to consider important ideas and concepts in a thoughtful way. (See the "Writing to Learn" section in your handbook for more information.)

One very effective writing-to-learn technique is **summary writing**. A summary is a compact and concise (to-the-point) account of learning material. It reflects your understanding of the material at hand, whether it's a reading assignment, a discussion, a project, or an important idea. To find out how to write a summary, see your handbook. (Refer to "Summary, writing the" in the index.) Put this information to good use in the activity below . . . and in your general course work.

Be a man or woman of few words.

WRITE: Write a summary paragraph for the multiparagraph essay test answer in your handbook. (Refer to "Essay test" in your handbook index. The model is on the last page in this section.) *Note:* Use the space below for the final copy of your work.

SUMMARY PARAGRAPH

_____

_____

_____

_____

_____

_____

_____

_____

_____

FOLLOW-UP • Share your work with a classmate. Pay close attention to the main ideas your partner included in his or her summary.

BUILDING ESSAYS

Multiparagraph Writing

WRITE: Read the three topic sentences following these directions. Then select four or five "Camel Facts" that support each topic sentence. Place a 1, 2, or 3 next to the fact, depending on the number of the topic sentence it supports. (The first two are done for you.) *Note:* You will not use every fact.

Topic Sentences:

1. Camels are hardy and amazingly self-sufficient.
2. People living in the desert depend on camels to help them survive.
3. However, camels can be troublesome to people.

CAMEL FACTS

2   can walk easily on soft sand where trucks would get stuck

1   carry lumps of fat in their humps that provide them with food

_____ stand six to seven feet tall

_____ sometimes spit at people when they're upset

_____ come in a variety of colors

_____ generally do not have the stamina to work hard for more than six months in a year

_____ can carry heavy loads (up to 330 lbs.) to places that have no roads

_____ are very strong and can pull plows in hard, dry soil

_____ can eat anything from hay to thorny twigs, even tent material if they have to

_____ have thick leather pads on their legs that act like knee pads on hot sand

_____ don't sweat, so they retain much of the water in their bodies

_____ have very long eyelashes

_____ kick frequently when they are upset or don't feel like working

The list continues on the next page.

■ Multiparagraph Writing *(Continued)*

_____ may turn around and try to bite a human rider

_____ on hot days, consume huge quantities of water (when it's available)

_____ give milk that is good for drinking or making cheese

_____ provide wool that can be made into clothing for humans

_____ can go for weeks, even months, without water if they have to

_____ baby camels are called calves

_____ may groan, wail, or refuse to stand up when asked to carry heavy loads

From List . . . to Essay

WRITE: Write a three-paragraph essay about camels, using the three topic sentences and related facts you've just identified in the list. (Refer to "Essay, School essay" in the handbook index for writing guidelines.)

(The space below is for planning or for your first draft. Write your final draft on your own paper.)

FOLLOW-UP • Share your finished product with a classmate. Note the similarities and differences in each other's work.

■ **Personal Essay Writing**

I find that amusing, don't you?

START-UP • For some types of writing, like **personal essays**, you don't have to look too far for writing ideas. Just about anything that interests you, amuses you, grinds your beans, or gets you thinking is a possible subject.

LIST: **Create a resource of writing ideas for a personal essay by retracing your steps for part of a typical school day (before school, during your morning schedule, during your afternoon schedule, after school, etc.). The model retracing below focuses on a student's actions before school. (Use the space at the bottom of the page for your work.)**

Model Retracing

Let's see. I got up, showered, dressed, and pulled my wallet and comb from my top drawer. Then I went to the kitchen for breakfast. I sat in my usual seat on the bus. I started worrying about the test I would have first hour. Our bus was early, so I had to wait outside, which made me mad.

Retracing Your Own Steps

_____

_____

_____

_____

_____

_____

_____

_____

_____

_____

Put your retracing to good use on the next page.

■ **Personal Essay Writing** *(Continued)*

Talent Search

LIST: On the lines below, identify three or four possible writing ideas from your retracing.

Special Note: The model retracing is printed in the handbook with possible writing ideas identified (in parentheses). Note how ideas were identified in the model before you do this in your own work. (Refer to "Essay, Personal" in the index. Once you turn to that section, look for "Selecting a Subject: What do I write about?")

_____

_____

_____

_____

_____

SELECT: Choose one of these ideas as the subject of your own personal essay. Writing guidelines are provided in the handbook before and after the model retracing. Also provided in this section is a list of different essay forms. (Use the space below for planning. Write the actual essay on your own paper.)

FOLLOW-UP • Share your finished work with at least one classmate. If you feel especially brave (and proud of your efforts), share your essay with a group of students or the entire class.

■ **Writing a Basic Analysis**

Go, Razorbacks. Go!

START-UP • Have you ever stopped to wonder why professional sports teams have the names they do? Why did somebody choose names like the Toronto Blue Jays, the Detroit Tigers, the Chicago Bulls, the Los Angeles Raiders, etc.?

SELECT: Choose a team and figure out the meaning of its name in the space below.
■ In the left column, list all the characteristics of the mascot the team was named after. (For example, a tiger is striped, furry, fast, ferocious, meat eating, and so on.)
■ In the next column, name the chief characteristics that are desirable in an athlete on that team. Draw lines between any characteristics that the two sides have in common. (For example, both are fast.)
■ Next, list all the characteristics implied by the name that are *not* meant to carry over to an athlete. (For example, badgers have flat heads and bad breath, but those aren't necessarily desirable qualities in an athlete.)

TEAM NAME: _____

Characteristics of the mascot:	Characteristics of a good athlete:	Characteristics of the mascot that don't fit the athlete:
_____	_____	_____
_____	_____	_____
_____	_____	_____
_____	_____	_____
_____	_____	_____
_____	_____	_____

WRITE: Put together all your thoughts on the subject and write a short essay (serious or funny) exploring the appropriateness of a particular team mascot.

Special Note: You might want to organize your writing in the following way: In the first paragraph, you could discuss the characteristics of a successful athlete in a particular sport. In the next paragraph (or two), you could discuss to what degree the team mascot reflects these characteristics or qualities.

■ **Writing Prompt**

Small Town / Big City

WRITE: After studying the prompt and the picture, write freely in the space provided for 5-10 minutes, comparing a small town to a big city. (Have another piece of paper ready in case you run out of room.)

Special Challenge: Develop this free writing into a comparison/contrast essay if you would like to continue exploring your comparison.

WRITING THE PHASE BIOGRAPHY

What was it really like?

START-UP • Through the ages, people have tried to imagine what it would be like to travel in time, from H. G. Wells' classic *Time Machine* to *Bill and Ted's Excellent Adventure*. During this unit, you'll be doing some time travel into the past and writing about people who have great stories to share with you. By the time you make it to the end of this journey, you will have written your first **phase biography**.

READ & REACT: **After reading the opening two pages of "Writing Phase Biographies" in your handbook, answer the following questions:**

HANDBOOK HELPER   Refer to "Biography, Writing a" in the index for this information.

➤ What is a phase biography?

➤ How is information gathered for this type of writing?

➤ Where (or how) can subjects be found for phase biographies?

➤ How did R. J. collect information for his writing?

➤ Why did R. J. choose to write about this person?

SELECT: **Whom would you like to write about in a phase biography? Try to select someone from a different generation—a grandparent, a neighbor, a teacher, an aunt, or a parent.**

■ Preparing to Interview

I'm so glad you asked!

START-UP • As you learned in the previous activity, one of the best ways to gather information for a phase biography is through interviewing. When you are planning an interview, keep the following points in mind:

- Write down as many questions as you can before the interview. (Base these questions on things you truly want to learn about your subject.)
- Decide what questions you will want to ask at the beginning of the interview.
- Include some questions that ask for personal opinions or reactions. *("What do you think about . . . ?")*
- Establish a time and a place for the interview.
- Be polite and courteous during the interview.
- Be prepared to take quick notes. (You can fill in later on.)

HANDBOOK HELPER	Refer to "Interviewing" in the handbook index for more information.

LIST: On your own paper, list questions you'd like to ask the subject of your writing. Make sure to plan your questions carefully.   It might be helpful to review sample questions written by another student named Erin Lovell. She used these questions when interviewing her grandmother.

- What major events have you witnessed in your life?
- How did these events affect you?
- What kind of activities or games did you enjoy as a child?
- What was a typical date like when you were a teenager?
- Who were the popular actors and singers when you were a teenager?
- What was school like for you?
- What changes have you seen in the rights of women or minorities?
- Who were your heroes? What were your dreams?

Special Note: From her interview, Erin gathered so much material, she felt like she could write a book about her grandmother. So she tackled the toughest part of writing a phase biography: deciding what information to use and what to leave on the "cutting room floor." She needed what the handbook calls a focus for her writing. Once Erin identified a focus, it was easy for her to decide what to include in her writing. (You'll find her biography on the next page.)

■ Reading and Writing a Phase Biography

READ: After reviewing her interview notes, student writer Erin Lovell decided to focus her writing on her grandmother's teen years. The section you are about to read focuses on two of her dates.

Strangers in the Night

An interesting topic sentence leads readers into the story.

Although my grandmother Lorraine Davis Lovell married young, she managed to have a few unusual dates before settling down with my grandpa. Here's how she remembered the first one.

"The only guy my father told me that I couldn't date again was Ralph Capone. I lived in the Irish Catholic part of Chicago, so I didn't know much about mobs. Well, I showed up at the door with Ralph and asked my father if I could go to dinner with him."

"Father said, 'Are you related to Al Capone?' "

Dialogue brings the first date to life.

" 'Yes, I am,' my date replied. 'He's my uncle.' "

"My dad let me go out with him, but when I got home he told me I could never go out with him again."

" 'Why?' I asked. 'Ralph was a nice guy.' "

" 'You could have gotten killed!' my father told me. I didn't understand, so he patiently explained that Ralph's Uncle Al was a head gangster!"

The only other date that Lorraine remembered wasn't really an official date. She was walking to a party with Jack Sherdon when a car pulled up to the sidewalk. A man jumped out of the passenger seat and held a gun up to them, telling Jack to empty his pockets.

This unusual experience stood out in the interview.

Jack did as instructed. In his pockets he had a dollar or so, but he also had Lorraine's new silver compact (a mirror with face powder in it). It was brand-new, and she was not about to let some stranger steal it.

After Jack handed him the money and the silver compact, the man threw the goods into the car.

"Could I have my compact, please?" Grandma asked.

The guy looked at her funny, then reached in and tossed it to her.

"Then he got back in his car and drove away."

WRITE: Now it's time for you to write the first draft of your own phase biography. Look back over your interview notes, think of a focus for your work, and start writing.

■ Reviewing and Revising Your Work

EVALUATE: The following checklist will help you review and revise your work. (Also refer to the "Writing Phase Biographies" chapter in the handbook for additional help.)

_____ **Organization:** Is the biography focused around a specific phase of the subject's life? Do all of the ideas in the writing follow in a logical order?

_____ **Detail:** Does the writing include enough specific information about the subject?

_____ **Style:** Does the biography begin with an effective topic sentence or opening idea? Does the paper read smoothly from start to finish?

_____ **Mechanics:** Has proper attention been given to neatness and accuracy? (Is any dialogue punctuated correctly?)

Additional Comments: (when reviewing a classmate's work)

_____ What did you especially like about the writing? (List one or two things.)

_____ What change would you recommend? (List at least one thing.)

FOLLOW-UP • Read your finished product out loud to your writing group or class. Sharing the stories of people you know and care about can be a very satisfying experience, so make sure that the subject of your writing receives a copy of the finished product.

■ Using the Venn Diagram

Two heads are better than one.

START-UP • Now that you have your first phase biography under your belt, it might be fun to take this form one step further by writing about two people. This will naturally lead to some interesting comparisons (and contrasts) between the two subjects.

LIST: **When it comes to comparing and contrasting, the Venn diagram is a very helpful graphic organizer. To make sure you understand how this graphic organizer works, complete the following activity:**

- In area 1, list three or four physical and/or personal characteristics unique to yourself.

- In area 2, list three or four physical and/or personal characteristics unique to a best friend.

- In area 3, list two or three qualities you and your friend have in common.

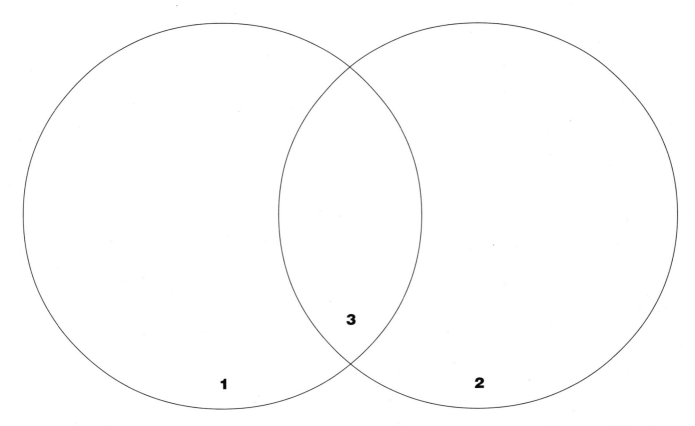

Special Note: It might be fun to have your best friend complete a Venn diagram following the same directions and then compare your results.

HANDBOOK HELPER   See "Venn diagram" in your handbook index for more information about this organizer.

■ Writing About Two Different People

START-UP • Note below how eighth grader Anne Morrissy used a Venn diagram to plan her phase biography about her maternal grandmother and her mother. (Anne asked each of her subjects the same questions during two different interviews.)

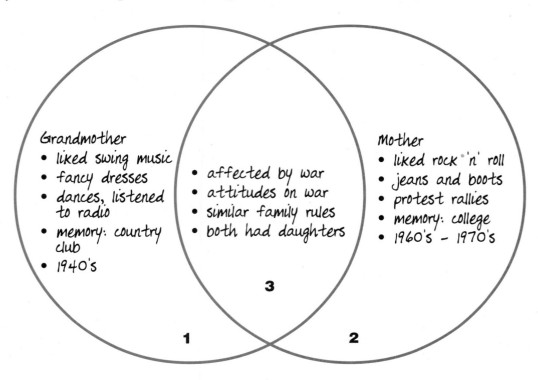

Grandmother
- liked swing music
- fancy dresses
- dances, listened to radio
- memory: country club
- 1940's

- affected by war
- attitudes on war
- similar family rules
- both had daughters

3

Mother
- liked rock 'n' roll
- jeans and boots
- protest rallies
- memory: college
- 1960's – 1970's

1   **2**

Special Note: As you will see in Anne's biography on the next pages, she organizes her writing according to the location of information in the Venn diagram, moving from the ideas in area **1** to the ideas in area **2** and so on.

SELECTING & COLLECTING: Select two people for your next phase biography. Then follow the planning steps as they are outlined below.

STEPS TO FOLLOW

- ● Select two subjects (from two different generations if at all possible).
- ● Generate a list of questions to ask each of them. (Ask them the same basic questions.)
- ● Set up an interview with both of your subjects (preferably at different times).
- ● Take careful but quick notes during each interview. (Be courteous.)
- ● Review your notes, and chart the main points in a Venn diagram.
- ● Use the diagram to help you find a focus for your writing. (You might focus on certain similarities or differences or some of each.)

■ Writing the Generations Paper: A Student Model

READ & REACT: As you read Anne Morrissy's model, pay special attention to the way she ties together the stories of her two subjects.

Like Mother, Like Daughter

Imagine an elegant ballroom decorated with starched white tablecloths at each table and fresh roses around the entire room. In the middle of the room, there is a huge dance floor made of marble; behind that, an orchestra plays a lovely tune, encouraging couples to dance before the night comes to a close.

The specific details in the opening paragraph grab the reader's attention.

Men are dressed elegantly in tuxedos and the women wear beautiful gowns of pink and peach and powder blue. Their arms are gloved up to their elbows and their hands rest daintily on the men's arms as they are led to the dance floor.

This was the world of my grandmother, Dorothy Gray, commonly known as Bitsey. This was her world before WW II changed everything. Balls were still held during the war, but the number of men in attendance dwindled to half.

During the forties, Bitsey remembered, the music that was popular then was called swing, and ballroom dancing was quite fashionable. Television had not yet been introduced, but they had radio. For a family afternoon, everyone would sit on the couch and listen to Jack Benny or a Sherlock Holmes mystery. If you preferred music, you could listen to the Lucky Strike Hit Parade.

Bitsey's parents had very strict rules. They always knew where she would be if she wanted to go out and with whom she was going. She had to be in by midnight or face certain death! If she was not at the dinner table by six, she didn't eat!

Eventually, Bitsey married and had two daughters, one of whom is my mother, Laurie Gray Morrissy.

The writer creates a smooth transition between the first and the second subject.

Although Laurie traded Bitsey's ballroom and Bitsey's ball gowns for bell-bottoms and boots, jeans and bandanas, the two women share definite similarities.

Both think their era is unique because of a war. In Bitsey's time, it was WW II, but in Laurie's era, the Vietnam War was raging in Southeast Asia. Laurie said this made people's futures uncertain because the boys weren't sure if they'd be drafted or continue with their educations. Once they were drafted, they weren't sure they would come back alive. Therefore they felt that they could do anything they wanted anytime they wanted because they might be drafted tomorrow and not return. (Interestingly,

The subjects shared similar feelings about the effects of war.

Specific quotations add life to the writing.

The conclusion ties everything together and extends the comparison into the future.

Bitsey said the same thing about her generation.)

The music of that generation was rock and roll and folk music. With the sixties and seventies came the freestyle dance craze where there were not set steps to learn. Everyone just "did their own thing."

Laurie's fondest memory of her youth is of her college years at Madison, Wisconsin. She and her friends would go to the political meetings, protest marches, and rallies together. She said the life she lives now is very different from the way she lived during that era. As she put it, "I have more responsibilities. I am less idealistic and more practical."

After college Laurie returned to live with her mother. Her rules were similar to the rules Bitsey had to live by when she was at home: Laurie, too, had to be at the dinner table by six or skip dinner, and she also had to tell her mother where she was going and with whom.

Two generations of my family, representing two very different eras: from the genteel forties to the wild seventies, both women share a bond, a closeness that cannot be explained simply by sharing the same blood. Similar influences, perhaps? That seems rather unlikely considering the different eras they belonged to. Perhaps, as they say, a woman really does turn into her mother. That would explain the similarities in mother and daughter, similarities that will most likely show up in me, and perhaps someday in my own daughter.

WRITE & REVISE: Write the first draft of your phase biography, using your interview notes, Venn diagram, and the model above as your guide. To revise your first draft, refer to the evaluating guidelines on page 26 in this unit. (When referring to those guidelines, remember you are working with two subjects instead of one.)

AFTER•THOUGHT This project may take some time; however, the discoveries you make about different people (and about yourself) during the process will make all of the work well worth the effort.

■ Writing About Other People

Amazing Stories

WRITE: I'll bet you've heard a number of amazing stories while completing the interviews for your phase biographies. Here are some other ways you might use that information.

1. Write your own historical fiction, a short story in which "you are there," living in that era. You could write a story as . . .

   - a flapper in the Roaring Twenties
   - a young boy growing up during the Great Depression
   - a foot soldier in World War II
   - a girl in a poodle skirt at a fifties sock-hop
   - a reporter at the first Beatles concert in the United States
   - a college student involved in an antiwar demonstration
   - a medic during the Vietnam War
   - (your choice?)

2. Make entries in an imaginary journal as if you were one of the people you interviewed. Choose a particularly exciting period in this person's life to write about.

3. Write a poem based on something you learned about one of your subjects.

4. Create an imaginary conversation between two people from two different generations.

5. Write a one-act play, enacting one of the best stories you heard in one of your interviews. Perhaps some of your friends could help you act it out for the class.

FOLLOW-UP • Share your creative writing with your classmates. You may choose to perform the writing in a readers' theater for your whole class.

WRITING A SURVIVAL STORY

Put to the Test

START-UP · Some people find out how strong or how brave they are when they are confronted by a problem. For example, a newspaper recently reported that a 12-year-old boy saved himself from drowning in a flooded cave by finding an oxygen pocket. It took both knowledge and skill for him to do this. The boy learned about oxygen pockets in his study of spelunking (cave exploring). He is a survivor.

In this unit you will think about your own survival skills, read an uplifting real-life survival story, and then develop a survival story of your own. In the process of developing your work, you will also learn about a very basic but effective story-planning strategy.

IDENTIFY: Use the following inventory to identify special skills you have developed or would like to develop that someday might help you survive.

SURVIVAL SKILLS INVENTORY

Skills I have developed

Example: **Learning how to swim**

When these skills would be most useful

Example: **Saving myself or others in a water-related accident**

_____ _____

_____ _____

_____ _____

Skills I would like to develop

Example: **Learning how to find oxygen pockets**

How I could use these skills

Example: **Surviving a flash flood while exploring a cave**

_____ _____

_____ _____

_____ _____

SELECT: Review the skills you have included in your inventory. Put a ✔ next to your most valuable skill and an ✘ next to the skill you would most like to develop. Then share your inventory with a classmate. (Have either of you seen any of these skills put to use in stories, movies, or real life?)

■ Reading a Real-Life Survival Story

READ: The following model is about Mitch Vitiello, a 12-year-old boy from New Jersey. As you read his story, you will see that Mitch had to employ a special survival skill. (This model, which is excerpted here, first appeared in the winter 1990 issue of *Shoe Tree*. It is reprinted with permission.)

Doing It Differently
By Mitch M. Vitiello

When I was eight, I noticed that I was different from the other kids. I made strange movements. It got to the point where they noticed. They started to laugh and look at me strangely. I felt bad inside, and sometimes I cried. I didn't know what was wrong with me. My parents didn't know. The doctors didn't know either.

Sometimes when I would be walking home from school, I would notice that my shoulder would fly up and hit my ear, or my feet would get this urge to kick. In class my head would jerk. I would try to control these movements but they would overrule me. It was like an incredible urge for them to get free and make me wiggle and jolt. There were times when my body would go absolutely nuts. I would stay in the house and not go out to play for days. I was thinking, "I'm going to die" when it got really bad. . . .

The years went by. I was nine, then ten, then eleven. All those years I developed new movements. Finally, when I was twelve, I was taken to special doctors who put things on my head, things that dug in and hurt, and I had tests and needles. The whole thing. And then they figured it out. I have Tourette's Syndrome. Tourette's Syndrome is a movement disorder which doctors think is caused by too much dopamine in the brain. It causes muscle movements, like tics, and vocal sounds which cannot be controlled. They think it is caused by a problem with the neurotransmitters in the brain which carry signals from cell to cell along the nerves. There are medicines to control severe cases, but they have bad side effects. You can leave it alone and deal with the condition and problems, such as people making fun of you. People with Tourette's can expect to live a normal life span. Even though the tics can make a person look like he is nervous, Tourette's is not a nervous condition. Some lucky people grow out of it completely after adolescence. I was told I have a mild case.

The summer I learned to deal with my problem was the summer I went to camp in Boston. It was 1987 and I was twelve and a half. I had looked forward to going for months, and the Tourette's seemed not to be acting up. Suddenly, just before leaving for camp, I had an allergy attack which always seemed to start the Tourette's problem. I was angry because I knew people would make fun of me at camp just like they did at school. It was frightening.

On the first day of camp, no one would even talk to me. I called home and told my parents that I had no friends. I was down and lonely. My mother wanted to come to pick me up. She thought the Tourette's was the worst it ever had been. It was. But my father said he had something very important to tell me. He said that I had to learn to deal with the condition, no matter how bad it got.

■ Reacting to a Survival Story

"If you act like it bothers you, it will bother other people. How you deal with your problem is how other people will deal with it. Act like it is nothing and soon they will forget about it."

I decided to take my father's advice. I thought about it all night, and I figured I had nothing to lose. My heart was in it. I went for it the next morning.

At breakfast I sat down at an empty table with my tray in front of me. My movements seemed worse than ever. My head kept on jerking back as I was trying to sip orange juice. Eating my eggs was a problem. My fork kept flying out of my hand.

As I kept eating, I saw five kids coming over to the table, and I knew it was time for me to try my new technique. First I had to act differently than I ever did before. I didn't move away from the table, and I didn't look down and try to pretend I was invisible. My thoughts were positive. I kept on telling myself, "I am powerful. I will not let this bother me."

As the other kids sat down, they noticed me right away. I saw them look at me and mumble to each other. I introduced myself. I said, "Hi, I'm Mitchell Vitiello. I'm from New Jersey. Where are you from?"

Two of the boys told me their names and where they were from. The other three just said "Hi." Already I knew it was starting to work. I was acting differently than I used to, and they were responding differently than other kids had. A boy named Seth asked me why I was moving like that. I thought to myself, "I must be strong. I must act like it doesn't bother me."

"Oh, it's just a condition that I have that acts up sometimes and makes me move differently. It's nothing major. It comes and goes. I can't help it. You'll get used to it," I said and smiled.

All the other kids went on eating and talking. I was overwhelmed at the outcome. I felt like letting out a big sigh of relief. I never felt that way before in all the years that I had the condition. Here I had acted as if I didn't care and the other kids didn't care either. My father's advice was good. I never expected it to work.

I learned a lot that summer. I felt good inside. Everywhere I went I used my new technique. It helped me tremendously. There were times when I was down, but not as down as I was before. Now I had courage to go out and do whatever I wanted to do in confidence that I could achieve it.

I changed the way I used to react, and people reacted in a different way to me. I have continued to use my father's advice and things have been a lot easier.

REACT: **Form responses to the following questions using your own paper. (Share your responses with your classmates.)**

_____ Why did Mitchell need to develop his particular survival skill?

_____ How would you describe this skill? (And did you list any skills like this one in your inventory on the previous page?)

_____ How did Mitchell put this skill to good use?

■ Using a Story-Writing Strategy

START-UP • The following planning strategy is helpful when you're trying to set a story in motion: (This strategy basically consists of filling in four basic story categories to help you organize your thinking.)

In most stories, there is (1) *someone* (the main character) in

(2) *someplace* (the setting) (3) *doing something* (the opening action), and

(4) *a problem occurs* (the conflict). (The main part of the story then

focuses on the main character's ability or inability to solve this problem.)

REACT: **Use the following planning guide to identify the four basic categories that initiate the action in the last half of the story "Doing It Differently." (The first blank is filled in for you.)**

In "Doing It Differently," (1) _____*Mitch*_____ is (2) _____
            (someone)   (someplace)

(3) _____ when (4) _____ .
            (doing something)   (a problem occurs)

(Because of this problem, Mitch decides to _____

_____

_____ .)

SELECT & COLLECT: **Select one of the skills from your personal inventory to use as a starting point for planning a story. Once you have a survival skill in mind, determine how you might build a story around it. Ask yourself who will use this skill and when or where it will become important to this person.**

Use the planning strategy above to help you get your story under way. Once you have identified at least three of your basic story categories—the main character, the setting, and the opening action—you're ready to start writing. (Use your own paper for your planning.)

Special Note: Your story can be based on a personal experience like Mitch's or on something you've heard or read about, but make sure to "fictionalize" your work in some way. (Change the names of the characters, place the story in a different setting, alter the action in some way, . . .)

■ Guidelines for Writing a Story

START-UP • Once you have a basic story idea in mind, the next step is to see how it develops in a first draft. But before you start your work, find out what your handbook has to say about the story-writing process.

REACT: Use the following guide to respond to the page entitled "Connecting: *Writing Your Story*" in the story-writing chapter in the handbook. (Provide at least two responses to each question. Afterward, share your work with a classmate.)

● How should you start?

● How should you continue?

● How should you end?

WRITE: Develop your first draft, keeping in mind some of the things you noted above about story writing. Remember to keep things as simple as possible in your writing. Once you get your story under way (*someone* is *someplace doing something*, etc.), focus the rest of your attention on one main action where a survival skill is needed.

Special Note: Don't expect things to work out perfectly in your first draft. It takes a lot of writing and rewriting to develop a well-made story.

■ Reviewing and Revising Your Story

EVALUATE: The following checklist will help you review and revise your survival story. (Use this same checklist to evaluate your classmates' work.)

_____ **Organization:** Is the writing organized around one main action? Does the story unfold in a logical and effective way, from beginning to end?

_____ **Detail:** Does the story contain enough detail to make it interesting? That is, does the story contain good descriptions, dialogue (if needed), and explanations?

_____ **Style:** Does the story start out effectively? Does it seem to have the right pace and movement? (Things shouldn't unfold too quickly.)

_____ **Mechanics:** Has proper attention been given to neatness and accuracy?

HANDBOOK HELPER Refer to the "Story Writing" chapter in the handbook for more revising tips. Look specifically for **"Connecting:** *Taking Inventory of Your Story"* once you turn to that chapter.

Special Note: If you're not sure how to word something or move your story along, you might also want to refer to published survival stories for ideas. Look at stories like "To Build a Fire" by Jack London and novels like *Hatchet* or *Haymeadow* by Gary Paulsen, *Julie of the Wolves* by Jean Craighead George, and *The Acorn People* by Ron Jones.

Special Challenge: After you share your work with your classmates, you might be ready to write another survival story. If that is the case, try writing a sequel (the next chapter) to the model story in the story-writing chapter in the handbook. The main character in this story is in need of a skill that will help her survive in her math class. Decide what that skill might be and how and when she could apply it.

■ **Writing a Quest Story**

Writing a Quest Story

WRITE: Here's a chance to develop another type of story called a quest, a story in which a young hero sets out to achieve or find something. In preparation for your story, complete the following plan.

1. Identify your character's **challenge**. (Maybe he or she sets out to make the basketball team.)

_____

_____

_____

2. Identify a **helper** for the main character. (Maybe an elderly neighbor helps him or her gain confidence.)

_____

_____

_____

3. Identify three (or more) possible **problems** that stand in his or her way. (Maybe the main character faces a penalty for arriving late to the first night of tryouts.)

_____

_____

_____

4. Identify a possible **ending** for your story. (Maybe the main character shows so much hustle, the coach can't help but keep him or her on the team.)

_____

_____

_____

FOLLOW-UP • Write your story, using the plan as a guide. (See "Story Writing" in your handbook for additional help.)

CAUSE AND EFFECT WRITING

Here Today, Gone Tomorrow

START-UP • What if I asked you the secret to your success (or lack of success) in school? In sports? Suppose I asked you what happened the last time you were late for something. Your response may start out something like this: "Because I was late for football practice, the coach made me run 15 laps around the track."

Cause and effect is an important part of our world. Read the newspaper or watch the nightly news—just about everything you see or hear can be explained in terms of cause and effect.

This unit will give you a better understanding of cause and effect writing. You'll have lots of opportunities to map cause and effect situations (or relationships). The thinking and writing skills you practice and polish here will help you in all of your school writing.

LIST: First you must practice thinking about a situation in order to discover its causes and effects. Consider clothing styles. They come and go so quickly—how does anyone keep up with them? In the space provided below, list as many causes and effects as you can think of for this fashion phenomenon. Let your imagination soar!   (We've given you a start.)

SITUATION:
Fast-changing clothing styles

CAUSES	EFFECTS
Designers need work.	*Staying in style can be costly.*

DISCUSS: Share lists with your classmates. After some discussion, choose what you believe to be the primary cause of changing fashions, as well as the most important effect.

FOLLOW-UP • Have you ever been swept up in a fad? Describe the fad and list its causes and effects. Use your own paper.

■ Mapping Out a Dream

Life is but a dream.

START-UP • What do you daydream about? What arouses your curiosity? What fires your imagination? Michael Crichton wondered what it would be like if dinosaurs could be cloned and wrote *Jurassic Park*. Space scientists dreamed about the stars and the planets and sent a team of astronauts to the moon. Composers wonder about different combinations of notes and instruments and create new songs and symphonies.

SELECT & COLLECT: Think of a dream that you have for the future. Imagine what might happen if that dream came true. Consider all of the possible effects. For example, you may dream of becoming a famous basketball player and then realize that, along with the fame and money, the strenuous practice schedule would take a big bite out of your social life. Choose your own dream for the future and fill in the following map.

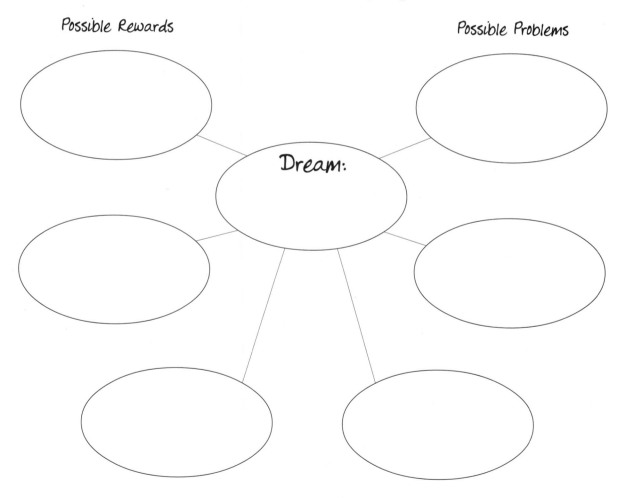

FOLLOW-UP • Exchange maps with a classmate. Ask your partner if he or she agrees with the rewards and problems you have listed.

■ Writing a Cause and Effect Paragraph

Dream on.

COLLECT & CONNECT: Reconsider the ideas in your dream map. (Do you have anything to add, especially details that will clearly explain your points?) Transfer all of your thoughts to the outline below, and state the conclusion you've reached about your dream.

I. THE DREAM:_____

II. THE EFFECTS:
    A. Positive (possible rewards)

        1._____

        2._____

        3._____

    B. Negative (possible problems)

        1._____

        2._____

        3._____

III. THE CONCLUSION:_____
    (your opinion after considering all of your dream's possible good and bad effects)

WRITE: Write a cause and effect paragraph, using the outline that you have just finished to organize your writing.

EVALUATE: The following checklist will help you review and revise your paragraph. (Use the same checklist to evaluate your classmates' work.)

_____ **Organization:**   Does the paragraph clearly state a dream, its possible effects, and a conclusion?

_____ **Detail:**   Is more information needed?

_____ **Style:**   Does the writing maintain a natural voice throughout?

_____ **Mechanics:**   Is the paragraph neat and accurate?

■ Planning a Cause and Effect Essay

From Another Angle

Now that you've practiced cause and effect paragraph writing, you're ready to try something new—the cause and effect essay. Simply follow the steps laid out for you on the next three pages.

LIST: Instead of considering possible effects of future happenings, look around you for recent actions or events that have affected you positively or negatively. You've gained or lost a friend. You've had an important discussion with a teacher. You and your classmates have gained or lost access to the computer lab. The city recently installed lights in the alley behind your house. List at least two or three actions or events in the space provided. (Share your ideas with a classmate.)

Actions or Events:

FRAMING YOUR TOPIC: Choose one action or event to be the topic for this writing activity. Put it into a starter sentence similar to either of the examples that follow. (Try using the sentence frames below, making changes as needed.)

Examples: **When** I met Sonja, **I** began to feel differently about school.

Because the city installed lights in our alley, **we now** make better use of it.

When _____ ,

I (we, they) _____ .

Because _____ ,

I (we, they) now _____ .

■ Collecting Your Thoughts for Writing

COLLECTING: List ideas (or write freely) about your starter sentence in the chart that follows. (Include as many related details as you can.) This chart will help you see your topic from different angles.

Three-Part Chart

BEFORE (What was it like *before* this action took place?)

DURING (*How, when, where,* and *why* did this action take place?)

AFTER (How have things *changed* because of this action?)

SO FAR SO GOOD • What you now have is a **cause and effect** essay in the making. You've identified an action that has *caused* some changes in your life. You've given this topic some shape in a starter sentence, and you've collected your thoughts about it in the above chart. Read on and learn how to put all of this work to good use.

■ Writing the Essay

So where do you go from here?

WRITE: Develop a CAUSE and EFFECT essay about your topic, incorporating the thoughts you collected on the previous page. The five steps below will help you do the necessary planning for a multiparagraph paper.

Easy Steps to Follow

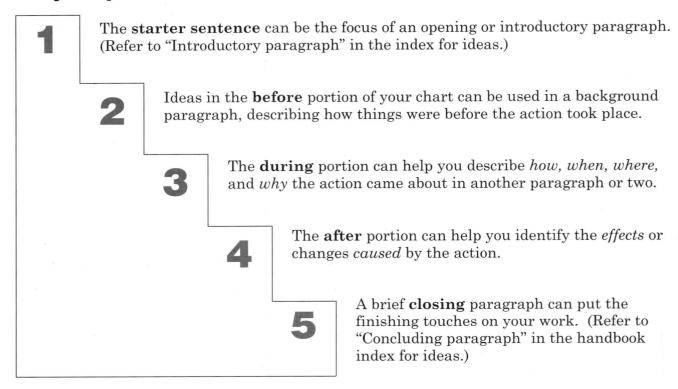

1 The **starter sentence** can be the focus of an opening or introductory paragraph. (Refer to "Introductory paragraph" in the index for ideas.)

2 Ideas in the **before** portion of your chart can be used in a background paragraph, describing how things were before the action took place.

3 The **during** portion can help you describe *how, when, where,* and *why* the action came about in another paragraph or two.

4 The **after** portion can help you identify the *effects* or changes *caused* by the action.

5 A brief **closing** paragraph can put the finishing touches on your work. (Refer to "Concluding paragraph" in the handbook index for ideas.)

FOLLOW-UP • Share the results of your work with a classmate. Then use the peer-editing questions on the next page to help you decide if your partner has effectively presented the causes and effects of a certain action.

■ Reviewing and Revising Your Essay

EVALUATE: The following checklist will help you review and revise your essay. (Use this same checklist to evaluate your partner's work.)

____ **Organization:** Is the event (cause) described clearly? Do the *effects* make sense to you? Does the concluding paragraph tie the important points together?

____ **Detail:** Are specific words used (active verbs, precise nouns and adjectives)? Is there enough information, or are you left with questions about anything?

____ **Style:** Does the writing flow smoothly and logically from start to finish?

____ **Mechanics:** Has proper attention been given to neatness and accuracy?

BEFORE PREPARING A FINAL COPY: Read your revised essay aloud to a classmate or family member. Listen carefully to your own words as you read. Do they say what you intended to say? Can you still improve your writing? Sometimes it will take three or four attempts before your writing says what you want it to say.

WRITING TO DEFINE

de•fine: *to determine or identify the meaning of . . .*

START-UP • Suppose I asked you to describe your typical morning routine. Your response would be automatic, wouldn't it? *"First I fall out of bed, stub my big toe on the way to the bathroom, and . . ."*

Now suppose I asked you to define the word "routine." Your job would be a little more difficult. What, for example, would be the first thing you would say about "routine"? Then what? You wouldn't know until you gave it some careful thought. To remember a typical morning "routine" is one thing; to define or explain a word like "routine" is another kettle of fish (another matter).

In this unit, you will be given many opportunities to plan thoughtful (and sometimes creative) definitions including a multiparagraph **extended definition**. The skills and strategies you practice here will help you with all of your writing in school, especially when you are asked to write paragraphs and reports and to answer essay-test questions.

■ NounBank

LIST: In the space provided below, create a resource of words to define by freely listing common nouns. (Common nouns are the ones that don't begin with capital letters.)

We'll get you started:

android
ankle
bagel
basket

FOLLOW-UP • Share your work with your classmates to see who was able to list the most nouns. (Make sure that all of the words listed are, in fact, nouns.)

■ Basic One-Sentence Definitions

START-UP • In most cases, defining a word means *classifying* it and then identifying its *basic characteristics.* Learn how to write basic definitions by completing the open-ended sentences in the box below.

HANDBOOK HELPER To complete these sentences, refer to "Definition, Guidelines for writing" in the handbook index.

Writing a Definition

Place the term you are defining into the _____

objects. Then add the special _____ that make this object

different from _____ .

        Term — A _____ . . .

        Class — is an _____ . . .

  Characteristic — that _____
               information.

Caution: Do not use the term or a form of it in your definition. *Example:*

"A _____ is a machine that _____ ."

Additional Examples:

Noun: _____android_____ **Basic Definition:** _____An android_____
is a high-tech machine designed in the form of a human being.

Noun: _____ankle_____ **Basic Definition:** _____An ankle is_____
the bone joint that connects the _____ _and_
the _____ . *(You should be able to fill in the blanks.)*

Discussion: In each of these examples, the noun is first classified ("An android is a high-tech machine") and then identified according to a special characteristic ("designed in the form of a human being").

■ Writing One-Sentence Definitions

DEFINE: Write basic one-sentence definitions for three of the words in your NounBank list. Make sure that your definitions follow the guidelines and examples on the previous page.

Special Note: If you find it difficult to define one or two of your nouns, substitute other choices. (Some words, as you will discover, are not easy to define in one sentence.)

1. Noun: _____ Basic Definition: _____

_____

_____

2. Noun: _____ Basic Definition: _____

_____

_____

3. Noun: _____ Basic Definition: _____

_____

_____

FOLLOW-UP • Afterward, compare your own basic definitions with the definitions provided in a dictionary. Also share your work with a classmate. As a team, put a ✔ next to the most effective definition in each other's list.

Fictionary Fun: Write one-sentence definitions for the following two words. (You won't know what these words mean, so make something up.) Upon completion, compare your definitions with the ones listed in a dictionary to see how close you came.

demijohn: _____

_____

fer-de-lance: _____

_____

■ Expanded One-Paragraph Definitions

START-UP • Let's suppose you (of all people) bump into Teewok on the way home from school, and he wants to know what is going on in the field across the street. (Teewok, by the way, is a stranger from a strange land.) You tell him that a baseball game is being played. He asks, "What is baseball?" Since you now know how to state a simple definition, you begin, "Baseball is a game played with a bat and ball between two teams on a field with four bases . . ." But before you go any further, you realize that you could go on and on with your "simple" definition. So you sit Teewok down on the curb and proceed to explain the game of baseball.

> *Moral of the story:* A simple definition can only do so much.

READ: **Carefully read the model definition that follows:**

> Braille is a system of communication used by the blind. It was developed in 1824 by a blind French student, Louis Braille. The code consists of an alphabet using combinations of small raised dots. The dots are imprinted on paper and can be felt, and thus read, by running the fingers across the page. The basic unit of the code is called a "cell," which is two dots wide and three dots high. Each letter is formed by different combinations of these dots. Numbers, punctuation marks, and even a system for writing music are also expressed by using different arrangements. The small dots, which may seem insignificant to the sighted, have opened up the entire world of books for the blind.

Special Note: The topic sentence of this paragraph is a basic one-sentence definition ("Braille is a system of . . ."). The sentences that follow expand and clarify this term and help create a more effective definition in paragraph form.

➤ *Now You Try*

DEFINE: Write an expanded one-paragraph definition for one of the nouns in your original list. This could be one of the nouns you defined in the last activity. Or perhaps you would like to define *baseball* for Teewok.

Remember: The topic sentence of your paragraph should be a basic definition of your word. Each sentence that follows should clarify or expand on this basic definition. (Space has been provided on the next page to help you plan and write your paragraph.)

■ One-Paragraph Definitions: Planning and Writing Sheet

TOPIC SENTENCE: On the lines below, provide a basic definition for the subject of your paragraph.

Noun: _____   Basic Definition: _____

_____

_____

COLLECTING DETAILS: Make a list of details supporting and expanding your basic definition. List as many details as you feel are necessary to complete your paragraph. (You might have to consult a magazine, a book, a dictionary, or an encyclopedia for information.)

Detail 1: _____

Detail 2: _____

Detail 3: _____

Detail 4: _____

Detail 5: _____

WRITE: Write the first draft and revisions on your own paper. (Remember to use the model on the previous page as a guide.)

HANDBOOK HELPER   Refer to "Paragraph, Basic parts" in the index if you need more help with your writing.

EVALUATE: The following checklist will help you review and revise your work. (Use this same checklist to evaluate your classmates' work.)

____ **Organization:** Does the paragraph begin with a clearly stated basic definition (the topic sentence)?

____ **Details:** Do all of the details contained in the paragraph support or expand upon this definition?

____ **Style:** Does the paragraph read smoothly and clearly from start to finish?

____ **Mechanics:** Has proper attention been given to neatness and accuracy?

■ Poetic Definitions

START-UP • So far you have dealt with definitions in a straightforward, matter-of-fact fashion ("A computer is . . . "). The feeling of a word, if not the basic meaning, can also be captured more creatively.

READ: The three poems that follow define words in creative ways, in ways that really only suggest meanings.

Styrofoam

Styrofoam—
a strange stuff
that bends, dents, and rips
when poked or pulled.

(A definition poem in
Write Source 2000)

Being down is
Lousy,
Ugh, but
Everyone is down sometimes.

(A title-down poem in
Write Source 2000)

pEAKs vALLEYs *LIFE!*

(A concrete poem in *Write Source 2000*)

REACT: Respond to these poems using the following directions as your guide.

_____ Put a ✔ next to the poem you like the best and an ✘ next to the one you like second best.

_____ In a few sentences, explain how one of these poems "defines" a word.

➤ *Now You Try*

WRITE: Write your own definition poem (or poems) using the models above as a guide, or working with a form and style completely of your own making. (The handbook section on poetry provides many ideas.)

■ Nouns in the Abstract

START-UP • Nouns are either abstract or concrete. **Concrete nouns** are physical words naming people, places, and things. **Abstract nouns**, on the other hand, have no physical qualities. That is, they can not be seen, heard, or touched. Abstract nouns name feelings *(anger)*, qualities *(wealth)*, and ideas *(democracy)*. Most of the nouns you have worked with up to this point have been concrete. In this activity, you are going to focus on abstract nouns.

HANDBOOK HELPER   Refer to "Concrete noun" and "Abstract, Noun" in the index for more information and examples.

LIST: **To prepare for your final definition assignments, create a resource of abstract nouns. To give this activity a creative twist, see how far you can get through the alphabet, listing abstract nouns. That is, see if you can list one or two abstract nouns starting with the letter A. Then do the same for the letter B, and so on. (If you get stuck, refer to a dictionary or thesaurus for ideas.)**

We'll get you started:

Anger, Affection
Bravery, Boredom
Confidence, C _____?
D

FOLLOW-UP • Compare lists with a classmate. Did you and your partner list any of the same abstract nouns? Which noun interests you the most in your partner's list? Which nouns interest you the most in your own list?

■ Defining in Dialogue Form

START-UP • In the following imaginary conversation, student writer Tony Yang tries to define the abstract noun *death* to an android trooper (an android, as you may remember, is a high-tech machine in human form). As you read this model, notice how the basic definition develops in context, as the conversation naturally unfolds.

What is . . . death?

Transcript of attempt to abort ticket. Officer EB0372-RX.
14:32.05   6/28/2026

Trooper: License and registration please.

Subject: Sir, I had to speed. I'm in a hurry. You see, my grandmother is dying in Detroit. I have to do 2,000 kilometers in, at the most, two hours. Please help me out; let me go.

Trooper: There is no excuse. You were going 1200 km/hr in an 800 km/hr zone. I must give you a ticket.

Subject: Don't you understand? My grandmother is DYING. El comprendé? DYING! This is my last chance to see her. Are you a robot or something?

Trooper: I am an android. "Dying" does not register in my memory banks. I must still give you a ticket.

Subject: Well that explains it. I'll try to make it clear to you what dying is. Please use logic. If you had a mother, which I know you don't, and she was to be turned off forever, how would you logically feel? You would want to see her for one last time. Right?

Trooper: Yes. Logically you are correct. My condolences would be with you were I capable of sending them to you; but I must still give you a ticket. There are no exceptions.

Subject: Why you *@!zx* robot! I explain it to you and you understand! Oh, just give me the ticket before I blow up.

Trooper: Whatever you wish, sir. Have a nice day.

➤ *Now You Try*

WRITE: **Select one of the abstract nouns from your list in the previous activity to define (or at least discuss) in an imaginary conversation. Use the model above as your guide.** *Note:* **Your speakers don't have to be futuristic or strange. (Do your work on your own paper.)**

■ Writing an Extended Definition

START-UP • An abstract noun is not easy to understand because it is not seeable or touchable. It figures then that it is also not easy to define. To properly define an abstract term like *love* or *freedom*, you must **extend** your thinking beyond basic definitions and consider the feelings and emotions associated with the word. An effective definition of an abstract term might include personal definitions, examples, famous quotations, descriptions, and perhaps even poetry.

REVIEW: **Below are a number of different methods writers use in extended definitions. Carefully read through this list.**

Methods for Developing Extended Definitions

1. **Include** a dictionary definition. (Choose the *best* definition for your situation.)

2. **Provide** a basic definition of your own and definitions stated by other people. (Make comparisons between all of the definitions.)

3. **Offer** a negative definition. (This is defining something by telling what it is not.)

4. **Identify** synonyms for the word. (Refer to a thesaurus for ideas.)

5. **Work in** examples or instances. ("I felt *freedom* when . . ." or "My mother felt *freedom* when . . .")

6. **Explain** the purpose or function of the word. (How, where, and when does this abstract term work?)

7. **Describe** the parts (and the sound) of the word. ("The root of *freedom* is 'free,' which means . . .")

8. **Compare** or **contrast** the word to related terms. ("*Freedom* is often linked to *democracy* because . . .")

9. **Use** the term in a simile or metaphor. (Or include a definition poem.)

10. **Quote** well-known people. (Refer to books of famous quotations for ideas.)

Note: You should not use all of these methods in one extended definition. The point is to make use of those methods that support your main feeling or attitude about the word you are defining.

READ: **On the next page, let's see how one student writer used some of these methods to write an extended definition about** *friendship.*

■ Model Extended Definition

Friendship

A personal definition of friendship is provided, followed by examples of true friendship.

Friendship is a word used to describe many different kinds of personal relationships. Many people are just acquaintances, yet they call it friendship. True friends know the difference. Other people are friends in school, and then after school, they go their own ways. True friends are not just "sometime friends."

The writer feels that the dictionary definition and common synonyms miss the point.

The dictionary defines friendship as "the condition or relation of being friends." But friendship could never be understood by simply reading a definition in a book. The thesaurus also tries to define friendship by using synonyms like "cordiality, fellowship, and brotherhood," but this also falls short of an acceptable definition. True, you will know what the word means technically, but you won't know what it actually is until you've experienced it firsthand.

More examples of true friendship are added.

To me, friendship is much more than two people simply knowing each other. It's knowing that someone will be there to share the good times and the bad. It's knowing that someone really does care about how you feel. It's a feeling that comes naturally and stays that way. Friendship is a strong innerfeeling that makes each day worthwhile.

Saved for last (and supported by a famous quotation) is the writer's most important example of true friendship.

But probably the most important thing about true friendship is that it lasts. It survives the fights, the jealousies, the misunderstandings. It doesn't wait for an apology: It says "That's okay" with a simple smile. Maybe the best single definition of friendship is one quoted by a famous writer who said, "You can always tell a real friend: When you've made a fool of yourself, he doesn't feel you've done a permanent job."

■ Selecting and Searching Your Subject

SELECT: Choose one of the words from your list of abstract nouns to define in an extended definition. (Choose a word that has special meaning to you, a word that you would like to think and write about.)

Subject of Extended Definition: _____

SEARCH: Explore your thoughts and feelings about your subject in a 10-minute free writing or clustering. Some of the discoveries you make here will help you write your extended definition. (Use the space below for your work, but have another piece of paper ready in case you run out of room.)

HANDBOOK HELPER	Guidelines for "Free Writing" and "Clustering" are listed in the index.

FOLLOW-UP • Review your free writing or clustering, underlining any ideas that you especially like. Look for personal definitions, examples of the word in action, reflective details (where you wonder about your subject), similes or metaphors, interesting descriptions, and so on.

■ Collecting Details

COLLECT: Use the following "Information Gathering Sheet" to collect ideas for your extended definition. (This sheet reflects the "Methods for Developing Extended Definitions" list on page 57 in this unit.)

INFORMATION GATHERING SHEET

Dictionary definition:

Personal definition:

Other people's definitions (parents, classmates, neighbors, etc.):

•

•

•

Negative definition (what your abstract word is not):

Synonyms and antonyms (from a thesaurus):

Important facts and figures (from reference books):

Quotations (famous people, literature, songs, etc.):

Special Note: Don't forget your own experiences, feelings (personal or poetic), observations (sights and sounds), and reflections (wonderings) related to your subject. You already collected some of these things in the last activity. Continue to gather more personal thoughts and feelings in additional free writing or clustering.

■ Collecting: Planning and Organizing Your Writing

START-UP • Once you have collected all of your "facts and feelings," your next step is to organize these ideas for writing. Start this process by identifying your main attitude about your subject. (The main attitude developed in the model is that true friendship cannot really be understood by reading basic definitions.)

FOCUS: What main feeling or attitude about your subject do you want to share? You may believe that . . .

- certain definitions and facts say more than others about your subject,

- personal experiences provide the best definitions,

- everyone has his or her opinion about this subject,

- or (your own idea)_____ .

ORGANIZING GUIDE

LIST: Use the following guide to plan and organize your writing.

Opening Paragraph: List below the information you plan on including in your first paragraph. Start with an attention-getting idea, fact, or definition.

Paragraph Two: List the main ideas you would like to include next. How about another person's definition, facts from a reference book, or a combination of ideas? (Whatever you include should support your main feeling about your subject.)

Paragraph Three: List the main idea or ideas you would like to include next.

Paragraph Four: List any additional ideas you would like to include. (End your paper on a strong note by saving some of your best information for last.)

(The length of your paper depends upon the amount of information you have to share.)

■ Connecting: Writing and Revising Your Extended Definition

WRITE: Write the first draft of your extended definition on your own paper. Spend a little extra time on your opening paragraph. Once you feel satisfied that it says what you want it to say, the rest of your writing will go much easier.

    Include ideas as you have them listed in the "Organizing Guide." However, don't be surprised if new ideas or a better way to present them comes to mind as you write. *Remember:* Your first draft is only your first look at your writing idea.

HANDBOOK HELPER	Refer to "Essay, School essay" in the index for additional writing guidelines.

EVALUATE: The following checklist will help you review and revise your extended definition. (Use this same checklist to evaluate your classmates' work.)

____ **Organization:**   Is the writing organized around a main feeling or attitude about the subject? Does the information in each paragraph seem to be arranged in the best possible order? Is this information easy to follow?

____ **Detail:**   Does the writing include enough supporting details (dictionary definitions, other people's definitions, synonyms, examples, etc.)?

____ **Style:**   Does the writing include effective opening and closing paragraphs?

____ **Mechanics:**   Has proper attention been given to accuracy and neatness?

Additional Comments: (when reviewing a classmate's work)

_____ What do you like best about this extended definition?

_____ What changes would you recommend?

PART II
Writing
Workshops

PREWRITING STRATEGIES

Selecting and Collecting Ideas

Most writers, even professional writers, agree that getting started is often the hardest part of writing. The **Prewriting Strategies** in this section will help you meet this challenge in new and interesting ways. You'll learn how to select writing ideas, how to collect details, and how to work together with classmates during the prewriting process.

After you have experimented with these strategies, you will undoubtedly settle on a combination that is just right for you. (Good writers rarely use only one strategy.) Many of the activities in this section can be used together to generate writing ideas. Keep this in mind as you work through these pages, and you will soon discover which strategies are right for you. Knowing more about getting started is the first step toward becoming an effective writer.

Special Note: Your handbook contains explanations and examples of many prewriting strategies. (Refer to index entries "Selecting, Topics" and "Searching and shaping a subject" for this information.)

Getting Started

User's Checklist

Check your progress as you work on these **Prewriting Strategies.**

☐ **Free Writing** • *"Here's what I'd do . . ."*

☐ **Clustering** • *From Pizza to World Hunger*

☐ **Listing and Co-listing** • *Superstars!*

☐ **Imaginary Conversation** • *"So what DO you use that X-ray vision for?"*

☐ **Brainstorming** • *"Boy, would I love to go there!"*

☐ **Story Starters** • *In Medias Res*

☐ **Observing and Recording** • *"Get on your knees . . . now!"*

☐ **Conducting a Survey** • *"Do you have a minute . . . ?"*

☐ **5 W's of Writing** • *Stranded!*

☐ **Inventory Sheet** • *Think about it!*

FREE WRITING

Free Writing *is just that: FREE. When you free-write, you let your ideas flow, freely—the way spilled ink would flow onto your paper. You don't need to worry about mechanics, paragraphs, or the order of ideas. You just go with whatever thoughts come into your mind, and you let them flow onto the paper.*

"Here's what I'd do . . ."

Most people complain about the things that are wrong in the world. Some, however, dream up an ideal model of the way things should be, and then aim for that ideal. That's what the people who founded this country did.

For a minute, pretend that you are in charge of putting together the perfect school. Writing quickly, and without pausing, describe the ideal you would aim for. Don't complain about what you don't like about school! Instead, "invent" a school with plenty to like—one where kids could learn interesting things in interesting ways. And try to be as daring and original as our nation's founders.

FOLLOW-UP • Share your writing with your classmates and teacher. Perhaps, under the guidance of your teachers, you could try to implement some of your ideas. You might collect the best ideas and send them to the school's board of education.

CLUSTERING

Whether you know it or not, you probably already use **clustering** *as a prewriting strategy. Maybe you've been asked to write an essay on Earth Day, and that gets you thinking about trees, which gets you thinking about the woodpecker in your backyard, and you wind up doing an essay about the importance of woodpeckers to the ecology. That's clustering.*

From Pizza to World Hunger

Do a cluster in the space below on the topic of food. Let one idea lead to another, adding whatever ideas, feelings, experience, or details that come to mind. (Look up "Clustering" in your handbook index for more information and a model.)

FOLLOW-UP • Go back and pick through your cluster for details you could include in a short paper on the subject of food. Share your ideas with your class. You'll be surprised to see how many topics are discussed—from "How to Make a Pizza" to "World Hunger."

LISTING AND CO-LISTING

Listing *and* **co-listing** *are two of the easiest prewriting strategies. All you have to do is open your mind and let the ideas march right out onto your paper. It's as easy as making a shopping list.*

Superstars!

▶ Working as quickly as you can, make a list of "The World's Most Interesting People." They can be personal acquaintances, historical figures, fictional characters, sports stars, or celebrities. Anybody from the president to Superman is okay!

▶ Pick one person from your list you would enjoy interviewing. If Barbara Walters had the chance to ask this very interesting person 10 questions, what do you think she would ask? For instance, she may ask Superman, "What is the single greatest advantage of X-ray vision?" Write your questions below.

1.

2.

3.

4.

5.

6.

7.

8.

9.

10.

FOLLOW-UP • Use these questions in the imaginary conversation activity.

IMAGINARY CONVERSATION

The next time you just can't get started on a writing assignment, try creating an **imaginary conversation**. *Let the two people carry on a conversation about your topic; keep it going for as long as you can.*

"So what DO you use that X-ray vision for?"

START-UP • Have you ever dreamed about being someone else? Say, a superstar like Michael Jordan or Winona Ryder? Or have you ever cast yourself into the leading role of a movie or book? Well, here's your chance to bring your fantasy to life! How? Read on!

▶ **Cast yourself into the role of the "interesting person" you picked to interview in the listing/co-listing activity. Write an imaginary conversation in which Barbara Walters interviews you, one of the most interesting people in the world. Answer at least 5 of your 10 questions, and continue the dialogue by writing the responses you think Barbara would have to your answers. Keep the conversation going for as long as you can. (Start below but finish on your own paper.)**

Question #1: _____

_____

_____

_____

Answer #1: _____

_____

_____

_____

Response #1: _____

_____

_____

_____

FOLLOW-UP • Go back and read your imaginary conversation. Use it as an idea source for a short essay about what you think this "interesting person" is (or was) really like.

BRAINSTORMING

Brainstorming *is just like listing, except you collect ideas from a group of people instead of from just one. When you brainstorm, ideas must be shared openly and without criticism. Even those that don't seem useful are written down and considered.*

"Boy, would I love to go there!"

▶ Together with your classmates or writing group, brainstorm for a list of places you would like to visit or have heard about on the news. You may choose places located anywhere in the world. Use the maps in the back of your handbook to generate ideas if you run dry.

▶ Choose one of these places and try to imagine what it would be like to be an eighth grader there. Brainstorm for a list of activities you think would be a typical part of your day. (If you don't know much about your choice, that's okay. Just use your imagination.)

FOLLOW-UP • Write a short story about a student who lives in this place. Include as much detail, both from your list and from other sources, as you possibly can.

STORY STARTERS

"Begin in the middle." As strange as this advice may sound, it is good advice, especially when you are writing a story. Start right in the middle of the action, just about the time the main character faces his greatest challenge. Later, you can fill your reader in on the details that landed your character in this predicament.

In Medias Res

In medias res is the Latin phrase for starting a story by jumping into the middle of the action. This old and respected writing strategy is especially effective when writing thrillers. For centuries people have "enjoyed" that delicious tingle that goes up the spine when they are introduced to a good ghost story on a moonlit night.

Barker had stayed after practice to work out for the third time that week. It was really no surprise that he had fallen asleep in the locker room, considering all the time he had spent running and lifting lately. As he headed down the darkened hallway toward the pay phones that hung in a tiny cove near the auditorium doors, he heard it. A sneering whimper accompanied by a scraping slither of something massive stopped his heart, and as he stood there trying not to breathe, he noticed that the temperature in the hallway had grown incredibly cold. Then came the smell . . . the awful, rancid smell that made him jerk back and gasp for air. And then he saw it . . .

▶ **Write a story starter for a ghost story—one filled with suspense and action rather than gory detail.**

FOLLOW-UP • Exchange your story starter with a classmate and finish one another's story. Remember, a story can end much differently than a reader expects. For instance, Barker's monster could turn out to be a lost Saint Bernard with bad breath.

OBSERVING AND RECORDING

Observing and recording *detail firsthand, and from a number of different angles, will give you plenty of fascinating information to draw from when you write. This activity will help you realize that the angle or perspective you write from determines how things "look" to a viewer (or reader). It will also help you master the prewriting strategy of observing and recording.*

"Get on your knees . . . now!"

Wherever you are at this moment, get on your knees! Do things look a little different when seen through the eyes of someone three feet tall (or is it three feet short)? Do you notice things you didn't "see" before? Observe and record as many details as you can.

Now get back in your seat. Continue to look for details, but try to see things that might not be so obvious at first . . . things you might see while lying on your back, or from the top of a seven-foot ladder. Try to find things no one else finds.

FOLLOW-UP • Exchange your work with one or more of your classmates. Did they notice things that you didn't?

CONDUCTING A SURVEY

*Some of the most valuable information a writer can collect (next to his or her own personal experience) is the experience and opinion of others. If you need only a small amount of information, you can simply conduct a few personal interviews. If, however, you need a wider range of opinions, you may want to do a **survey** or an **opinion poll**.*

"Do you have a minute . . . ?"

Begin by thinking of a topic you would like to know more about, especially how other people feel about it. (The list below might give you some ideas.) Then put together a list of questions you would like to ask and run off several copies. *Helpful Hint:* **You will need to decide who you're going to survey before writing your questions. Whose opinions are you seeking?**

Survey Idea List
- TV/MTV/Cable TV
- Current trends/fashions
- A school or community problem or issue
- A national or world event

FOLLOW-UP • Write a summary of how the people responded to your survey. Did most respond freely and openly? Did any have trouble understanding your questions? Did the results surprise you? What did you learn about your topic and about conducting surveys?

5 W's OF WRITING

A prewriting strategy commonly used for factual writing is the **5 W's.** *By answering* **who, what, when, where, why** *(and sometimes how) about your subject, you will usually have plenty to write about.*

Stranded!

Have you ever been stranded in a place you didn't want to be? Maybe your parents forgot to pick you up after a ball game, and you were left stranded long after everyone else had gone home. Maybe you locked yourself in a room and found out later, when you wanted to leave, that the lock was jammed and no one was left in the building to unjam it. What's *your* story? (Use the 5-W's strategy to get you started.)

Who?

What?

When?

Where?

Why?

How?

FOLLOW-UP • Now, using the information you've gathered, write a short description of the time you were stranded.

INVENTORY SHEET

After you have selected a subject to write about (but before you do too much writing), it is usually a good idea to stop and think about your subject and how well it matches up to your writing assignment and your reader. The **inventory sheet** *below should help you think things through.*

Think about it!

Begin by reading the first two pages in the "Collecting" section of "The Writing Process." (See "Collecting" in your handbook index.) Then answer the questions below using a current (or recent) writing assignment:

1. What am I required to do in this writing?

2. Does my subject match up to these requirements?

3. How do I feel about the subject?

4. How much do I know about this subject?

5. Is my subject too general or too specific?

6. Who am I writing this for?

7. How much do they already know about this topic?

8. How can I get them interested in my ideas?

9. In what form (story, essay, poem) should I present my ideas?

10. Can I think of an interesting way to start my paper?

FOLLOW-UP • Use these (and other) questions each time you write. Obviously, you do not need to write down an answer for each; simply "think about it."

FORMS OF WRITING

You'll like what's inside.

The **Forms of Writing** section is a trick-or-treat bag containing a wide assortment of writing activities. You'll be asked to start a personal writing program and to write about a joyous experience. You'll be asked to write a lead paragraph for a news story and develop a plan for a short story. You'll also be asked to praise an object and develop your own manual of home cures. Get the picture? There is a lot here for you to enjoy.

These special activities engage you in personal writing, subject writing, and creative writing—the three major categories of writing covered in your handbook. Taken as a whole, they will expand your writing knowledge, fine-tune your communication skills, and satisfy your creative sweet tooth.

Special Note: Your handbook "catalogs" a variety of important writing forms. Review the table of contents and see for yourself.

Getting Started

User's Checklist

Check your progress as you work on these **Forms of Writing**.

- [ ] **Personal Journal Writing** • *Preparing for Liftoff*

- [ ] **Eulogizing an Object** • *The "Kernel" made popcorn an experience.*

- [ ] **Writing Anecdotes** • *Slices of Life*

- [ ] **Writing Leads for News Stories** • *Extra! Extra!*

- [ ] **Developing a Manual** • *"Take two elderberries and call me . . ."*

- [ ] **Writing a Book Review** • *That's my kind of book!*

- [ ] **Developing a Character Sketch** • *I've got you pegged!*

- [ ] **Building a Story** • *A-questing we will go . . .*

FOLLOW-UP • We encourage you to experiment with a wide variety of writing forms—both inside and outside of school. Such experimenting will make you a "writer for all reasons." (Refer to "Writing, Forms" in the handbook index for ideas.)

PERSONAL JOURNAL WRITING
Preparing for Liftoff

START-UP • By the time a team of astronauts lifts off for space, they've been put through months of training. They are well prepared to conduct their business effectively and efficiently from countdown to splashdown. Nothing is left to chance.

We'd like you to start a personal training program—not one that will literally send you into space, and not one that is overly challenging, but one that *will* help you inside and outside of school. We'd like you to start a personal writing program. There's no better way to meet any writing challenge than to have plenty of training.

▶ **For a good starting point, read "An Invitation to Writing" in the handbook. (See the first page in "Writing to Learn.") Then follow the countdown at the bottom of the page and actually "lift off" into your training program. (Use the space below for your writing, but have another sheet of paper ready in case you have a lot to say.)**

FOLLOW-UP • Congratulations, your writing program is under way. Be sure to continue writing—tomorrow, the day after that, next week, . . .

EULOGIZING AN OBJECT

The "Kernel" made popcorn an experience.

▶ Eulogize (or praise) the "passing" of a beloved machine, appliance, toy, or other object by completing the following paragraph frame.

In memory of my beloved _____ ,

I would like to express these few parting thoughts. I first met _____

in _____ .

From that time on, we _____

_____ .

This loyal friend made _____ .

I'll never forget the time _____

or the time _____

_____ .

I can only think of one time (or two) when my pal didn't serve me to the best of its

ability. One time _____

_____ .

Another time (optional) _____

_____ .

But those times were exceptions. All in all, _____

has served me as well or better than _____

or _____ . I only hope that all of my future

_____ serve me as well. So long, dear friend. May

you rest in peace in the nearest _____ .

FOLLOW-UP • Share your work with a classmate. Then write your own eulogy about the passing of a time in your life, the passing of a memorable day, the passing of an old school or neighborhood, the passing of . . .

WRITING ANECDOTES

Slices of Life

START-UP • A lot of specific details and numbers don't have a lot of staying power with most readers—unless, of course, the details are real eye-openers. It's little stories or **anecdotes** about people that stick with readers. These brief "slices of life" communicate important ideas in a personable way; they make your writing appealing and lively. (See your handbook for more about anecdotes.)

An Anecdote in Action

You've probably heard time and time again that writing should be clear and to the point. This time-honored rule takes on much more meaning when it is supported by the following anecdote (a simplified version of the original):

A friend of Benjamin Franklin wanted a sign to announce his new business. He started with "John Thompson, Hatter, makes and sells hats for ready money" with a little picture of a hat next to these words. One of his friends said "Hatter" was repetitious with "makes hats" so it was cut. Another friend suggested he cut the word "makes" since selling is the important thing. A third friend said "for ready money" wasn't needed because no one sold on credit. A last friend said "sells" could be cut as well. After all, no one expected Mr. Thompson to give the hats away. Then "hats" was cut because there was a picture of a hat on the sign. What was left? "John Thompson" and the picture were all that remained. (But they were enough to communicate a simple, clear message.)

Now you try!

▶ **Think of an anecdote that was told to you by someone older and wiser to prove a point. Or ask one of your elders if he or she knows one. (An elder could be a parent, grandparent, neighbor, teacher, etc.) Then on your own paper, write this little story and the point it makes.**

Special Note: If you can't "find" an anecdote, create one of your own. Think of something that has happened to you or to someone you know that proves a point. Or write your own version of the Ben Franklin anecdote or a new version of a story like "The Hare and the Tortoise" or "The Little Engine That Could."

FOLLOW-UP • Share your anecdote with a classmate or writing group. Those stories that "work" really well should be shared with the entire class.

WRITING LEADS FOR NEWS STORIES

Extra! Extra!

START-UP • Most news stories begin with a power-packed **lead paragraph** that summarizes the main points of the story. The main points answer the 5 W's and H (*who, what, where, when, why,* and *how*) of the story. Lead paragraphs are generally no longer than three or four sentences. (Refer to "News story, writing" in your handbook index for more information.)

Study the following headline:

Students claim UFO lands on school.

Now make up answers to the 5 W's and H for a news story with this headline. (Use the space provided below.)

Who?

What?

Where?

When?

Why?

How?

LEAD: With the "facts" you have gathered, write a clear lead paragraph for this news story. (Use your own paper.) *Special Note:* If you're really on a roll, write the rest of the story. Or, if you have trouble writing a lead paragraph about the students' UFO claim, change the headline to meet your needs.

FOLLOW-UP • Write an original headline on a separate piece of paper. Make it a real attention getter. Then exchange papers with a classmate. Write a lead paragraph for each other's headline. (Share your results.)

DEVELOPING A MANUAL

"Take two elderberries and call me . . ."

START-UP • Let's suppose our ailments and illnesses were all treated with home cures as they once were in remote areas of our country. Home cures primarily consisted of different mixtures of plant life (including flowers, roots, fruits, leaves, and seeds) that were cut, ground, mixed, pressed, dried, and so on. This mixture might be sipped in a tea, swallowed, rubbed in, applied in a poultice (heated mass), or even tied around the neck.

Back to Basics

If someone would open your back-to-basics home-cure manual, what treatment would it prescribe for the common ailments listed below? (The first one is done for you.)

Note: It might be helpful to work on this activity with a partner if your teacher allows it.

SKIN BURN: Mix the whites of three eggs with the flowers of five freshly picked dandelions. Cool this mixture in the creek for an hour. Then rub it on the burned area. Reapply when necessary until the pain disappears. *Note:* If no dandelions are available, use skunk cabbage (if you can stand the smell).

HEADACHE:

TOOTHACHE:

COMMON COLD:

WARTS:

FLU:

Special Note: Consider designing a booklet of home cures, complete with illustrations.

FOLLOW-UP • If you enjoyed developing a home-cure manual, try compiling a list of your favorite down-home recipes and get to work on your own back-to-basics cookbook.

WRITING A BOOK REVIEW

That's my kind of book!

START-UP • In a book review, you have to do more than tell your audience what the book is about (although you should do some of that). You have to state your reaction to the book (your opinion about it) and back it up with specific facts and details from the text.

Charting a Review

▶ **Use the chart that follows to collect your thoughts and feelings about a book you've recently read. If at all possible, choose a book of fiction for this activity. You may, however, choose a nonfiction title if you have a "hot" prospect in mind. (You may even review your handbook if you are so inclined.)**

General Observations About the Book

Pay special attention to the following ideas:
- *how you came to read this book,*
- *how it compares to other books of this type or other books by this author,*
- *how the plot unfolds (be brief),*
- *how you felt about the book at the beginning, in the middle, and at the end,*
- *plus any other general thoughts or feelings you may have.*

Example Observation: *I read anything related to science fiction, especially books by*

Madeleine L'Engle.

_____

_____

_____

_____

_____

_____

_____

_____

_____

* *The chart continues on the next page.*

What do you like about the book and why?

   Pay special attention to specific features of the plot, setting, theme, and characters. (Refer to the second page in "The Book Review" section of your handbook for ideas.)

Example Observation: *Having Johnny jump into the burning church was a great way to add drama to the plot.*

_____

_____

_____

_____

_____

What don't you like about the book and why?

   Again, pay special attention to specific features of the plot, setting, theme, and characters.

Example Observation: *Becky's decision to ask John to the dance seemed totally out of character for her.*

_____

_____

_____

_____

_____

Compiling a Review

▶ **Write a review of this book. Here's a possible format: In your introductory paragraph, focus on one or more of the general observations as a lead into a general opinion statement (thesis) about the book. In the next paragraphs (at least two), point to specific things that you liked and disliked in the book. Make sure that you support your ideas with specific references from the book. Bring your review to an end with a brief closing paragraph.**

FOLLOW-UP • Exchange your review with a classmate. Discuss the effectiveness of each other's work.

DEVELOPING A CHARACTER SKETCH

I've got you pegged!

START-UP • There is always much more to a person than his or her "cover" or appearance. There are, in fact, pages of thoughts and feelings that have to be read and reread before a person can be fully appreciated. This is something you should never forget . . . well, almost never. You are officially relieved of this responsibility for the following activity (but only for the following activity).

Give each of the "characters" below some life by listing two of his or her outstanding PHYSICAL CHARACTERISTICS—*a character's eyes might be described as studious or thoughtful*—and two PERSONAL CHARACTERISTICS—*a character might carry a lifetime supply of sensitive feelings.* (Work with a partner if your teacher allows it.)

Special Note: (Refer to "Character sketch" in the handbook index to help you develop your work. Once you turn to that section, look specifically for "Collecting: Gathering Details.")

● Muffy Ann McLittle

● Constance Reformer

● Bull Armstrong

● Eliot Sinclair

● (A name of your own choosing)

● (A name of your own choosing)

FOLLOW-UP • Place one of these characters in a specific setting (on a bus, in the gym or library, etc.) and describe his or her actions and thoughts accordingly. Use the traits listed above to help you develop your writing. (Share your results.)

BUILDING A STORY

A-questing we will go . . .

Here's a chance to develop a story in which a young hero sets out to achieve or find something. In preparation for your story, complete the following plan.

1. Identify your character's **challenge**. (Maybe he or she sets out to make the basketball team.)

    _____

    _____

2. Identify a **helper** for the main character. (Maybe an elderly neighbor helps him or her gain confidence.)

    _____

    _____

3. Identify three (or more) possible **problems** that stand in his or her way. (Maybe the main character faces a penalty for arriving late to the first night of tryouts.)

    _____

    _____

    _____

4. Identify a possible **ending** for your story. (Maybe the main character shows so much hustle, the coach can't help but keep him or her on the team.)

    _____

    _____

    _____

FOLLOW-UP • Write your story, using the plan as a guide. (See "Story Writing" in your handbook for help.)

REVISING WORKSHOPS

Connecting and Correcting Your Ideas

Writer Bernard Malamud once had this to say about the process of writing: "The idea is to get the pencil moving quickly." This is good advice for all young writers. Writing freely and rapidly, especially at the beginning of a writing project, will often unlock some of your best thinking. Once you hit upon an interesting idea, you are on your way. That is, you are ready to see what you can discover in a first draft.

The **Revising Workshops** in this section focus on the connecting step in the writing process—that is, the step when you are ready to improve your first drafts so they speak more clearly and completely.

These workshops will help you review first drafts, support opinions, add specific details, and use sensory details. (See "Revising" in the handbook index for helpful information related to this important step in the writing process.)

Getting Started

User's Checklist

Check your progress as you work on these **Revising Workshops**.

☐ **Peer Reviewing** • *Three Before Me*

☐ **Group Advising and Revising** • *You're all in "this" together.*

☐ **Reviewing a Paragraph** • *My "Collectibles"*

☐ **Reviewing and Revising a Paragraph** • *The Big . . . and the Little of It*

☐ **Supporting Opinions** • *Prove it!*

☐ **Adding Specific Detail** • *Food for the Birds*

☐ **Using Sensory Detail** • *It makes sense.*

FOLLOW-UP • Here's some general writing advice: Evaluate your writing progress throughout the school year by exploring your thoughts and feelings about your writing in a journal. This is a great way to keep track of your growth as a writer.

PEER REVIEWING

START-UP • It's not easy to look clearly at the first draft of a writing assignment, especially if you've put a lot of time and effort into getting your ideas down on paper. You're too personally involved with it. You need someone else to review your paper for you—someone you trust, someone who knows you and knows the writing assignment. That someone obviously is one of your classmates.

Ideally, more than one classmate will review your first complete draft. (That's why the title of this activity is "Three Before Me." When you need to figure out what's good and what's bad in your writing, three heads are better than one . . . or two.)

Three Before Me

► **Exchange first drafts of a writing assignment among the members of your writing group or class so that each draft is read by three different classmates. After you read each draft, complete a simple review sheet like the one below on your own paper or use a review sheet provided by your teacher. Make additional comments clear so the writers can make good use of them.**

REVIEW SHEET	Redo	Improve	Leave
Opening: *Is the subject clearly stated? Does the opening grab your attention?*			
Body: *Do all the details in the body relate to and support the subject?*			
Closing: *Does the writing end naturally after the last important point is made?*			

What I especially like: (Maybe some part is funny, surprising, or especially attention getting. Maybe you like the sound of a passage or a particular choice of words. Or maybe the writing is especially honest and sounds just like the writer.)

Questions: (Maybe some parts seem unclear or confusing. Maybe more detail or explanation is needed in certain parts. Maybe other parts don't seem to fit. Maybe some of the thoughts don't read smoothly, or the words don't seem very exciting.)

FOLLOW-UP • Study your classmates' comments. Then review your writing. See how your observations match their thinking, and then plan your next writing moves.

GROUP ADVISING AND REVISING

START-UP • Many students organize themselves into groups to help each other with their writing. (It's best to start small with two or three members.) Let's suppose that's the route you and your classmates plan to take. What should you do first, second, and third? Read on and find out.

You're all in "this" together.

▶ Pair up with a classmate (or work in threes), and then turn to the section on "Group Advising" in your handbook. One person should read the guidelines listed on the first page of this section. The partner should follow along and listen carefully. (Reverse roles and read the guidelines again if either of you feel that you missed any important points.)

Then close your handbooks, and in the spaces provided below, each of you "sum up" what you learned about the responsibilities of writers and group members.

The Writer's Responsibilities:

The Group Members' Responsibilities:

AFTER • THOUGHT Discuss the results of your summaries. Also compare your work with the guidelines in the book.

FOLLOW-UP • Put into practice what you have learned the next time you share your work in a writing group.

REVIEWING A PARAGRAPH

My "Collectibles"

▶ **Read the following paragraph. Then tell what you think are the paragraph's strengths and weaknesses in the spaces provided. Make at least one observation in each category. (The "Commenting on Writing" checklist at the end of "Group Advising" will help you make your remarks. Also refer to your handbook for information about topic sentences.)**

I sat down at my desk in my room and really intended to do my English assignment, but then I started looking at my desk and thought about all of the neat things that I had collected throughout the years. My desk is its own little world, a world of collectibles. To me none of it is junk; I certainly wouldn't call it that anyway. All types of little doodads from my past presented themselves to me and my interest was spurred. There were all sorts of great things in that desk! They seemed to be "asking" to be arranged and neatened up. But what a challenge it was going to be! Maybe it was the thought of the challenge that interested me, or maybe it was an excuse not to do my homework. Whatever the case, I organized my desk.

Topic sentence: *(Does the topic sentence state a specific subject plus a specific attitude or feeling about that subject?)*

_____

_____

_____

_____

Purpose and voice: *(What is the writer trying to do in this writing? Does the writing sound honest and sincere?)*

_____

_____

_____

_____

Content and form: *(Has the writer included enough information and presented it in a clear way?)*

_____

_____

_____

_____

Sentence style: *(Are the sentences smooth reading, clear, detailed, etc.?)*

_____

_____

_____

_____

Overall strengths and weaknesses:

_____

_____

_____

_____

AFTER • THOUGHT Share your observations with your classmates. *Remember:* Not everyone "sees" the same things in a piece of writing.

FOLLOW-UP • Make two improvements in the original paragraph. (You might re-write the topic sentence or add detail in a certain section.) Share your results.

REVIEWING AND REVISING A PARAGRAPH

START-UP • A paragraph is big enough so that you must be concerned about the working parts associated with any longer composition: the beginning, middle, and end. It's also small enough so that you must be just as concerned with word choice, variety, and the "sound" of individual sentences.

The Big . . . and the Little of It

Read the paragraph below; then answer the questions that follow.

(1) It was the winter of our fifth grade. (2) What would start out as a few friendly snowballs tossed through the air would somehow end up as a mass snow fight. (3) Almost every day we had a great time playing in the snow. (4) Snowballs whizzed past unprotected heads, and face washings came from every direction. (5) After recess our wet hair dripped on the desktops while snow from our pant legs melted into puddles on the floor. (6) The hallway smelled like a wool-dyeing factory. (7) Sixth graders pushed past our classroom on their way to band practice. (8) The teachers and the principal didn't like our wet recesses and told us so, but we always seemed to forget what they said. (9) We were having too much fun dodging snowballs to listen to reason.

1. **Topic sentence: Reword** the topic sentence (in this case, the first sentence) so that it tells more exactly what this paragraph is about. (See "Paragraph, Topic sentence" in your handbook index for help.)

   _____

   _____

2. **Unity:** All sentences in a paragraph must tell us more about the subject of the topic sentence. **Draw** a line through the sentence that is off the topic.

3. **Organization:** All the sentences in a paragraph should be arranged in a logical order. **Find** one sentence in this paragraph that is out of order, and put it in its proper place by listing the correct order of sentences (by number) below.

   _____

4. **Closing sentence:** The last sentence of this paragraph brings the writing to an effective ending, but writers always look for an even better way of saying something. **Write** your own final sentence below. (See "Paragraph, Basic parts" for help.)

   _____

SUPPORTING OPINIONS

START-UP • How do you react to the following statement? "Students do not have enough time for homework because they have better things to do." It's not a very convincing claim, is it? Some students may have little time for homework, but "having better things to do" is far from a solid or supportable reason for this claim. Whenever a writer makes a statement of opinion, he or she must support it with clear and provable facts. This is a basic principle for all types of persuasive (and informative) writing.

Prove it!

Read the paragraph that follows. (It is a rather "defenseless" persuasive paragraph.) Afterward, strengthen the writing by adding clear and provable facts that support the topic (first) sentence. Use your own paper.

Students do not have enough time to do homework. Students need time to do other things with their friends. All sorts of activities take up time after school, too. Students may also be taking lessons or other classes after regular school ends. Students are overloaded.

In Search of Details

Use the questions that follow to help you find facts to support the paragraph's topic sentence.

- ❑ How often do students get homework?
- ❑ How many teachers assign homework?
- ❑ How long does it typically take students to do their homework?
- ❑ What "other things" take up after-school time?
- ❑ What organized activities take up after-school time?
- ❑ What lessons or other classes do students take?
- ❑ Why are students overloaded?

TIP Don't worry if your writing turns out to be longer than one paragraph. Also, don't worry if you have to work in one or two completely new ideas or cut some of the original ones. (See "Persuading, Guidelines for writing" in your handbook index for help.)

FOLLOW-UP • Share your writing with a classmate. Check each other's work for examples of fuzzy thinking. (See the last two pages in "Thinking Logically" for help.)

ADDING SPECIFIC DETAIL

START-UP • What should you do with a first draft that *really* lacks flavor and appeal? Well, you have two basic options: You can throw it to the birds and start over, or you can try to make the draft more appetizing. We generally recommend the second course of action. However, don't waste too much butter and cream on *every* first draft. Sometimes it's easier and more productive to start from scratch than it is to deal with writing that needs a lot of work.

Food for the Birds

How can you save a first draft from the bird feeder?

For one thing, you can use more specific details in sections that seem too general or vague. By specific details, we mean words that create a clear picture in the reader's mind. Read through the section on "Improving Your Writing" in the handbook for information about adding specific detail to your writing. (Refer to "Word choice, Specific" in the index for the location of this section.) Make good use of what you learn about specific detail when you work on the following exercise.

▶ **The following sentences express very general statements. Rewrite each one so it is more specific, vivid, and inviting. Consider using more exact nouns, lively verbs, and a few colorful adjectives and adverbs.**

Caution: Try not to stuff your sentences with too much information. Each one should contain just enough detail to whet a reader's appetite so he or she will want to read on.

Example: The man parked the car in front of the restaurant.

The stranger maneuvered the rusty hatchback in front of Sally's Burger Barn.

1. The man got out of his car.

_____

_____

_____

2. He walked into the restaurant.

_____

_____

_____

_____

3. The diners looked at him.

_____

_____

_____

4. The man sat at the lunch counter.

_____

_____

_____

5. A waitress gave him a menu.

_____

_____

_____

AFTER • THOUGHT   Exchange sentences with a partner.   Make note of specific words or details that you like in each other's work.

FOLLOW-UP • Continue writing this story if you like where it's headed. Or, for more practice using specific detail, create your own general story starter for a classroom exchange. (Use the space above for your work.)

USING SENSORY DETAIL

START-UP • Sensory details come from the writer's senses (smell, touch, taste, sound, and sight). This type of detail is very important in descriptive writing.

It makes sense.

Provide sensory details that could be substituted effectively for the words in parentheses. Note that one column of new sensory details is listed for you. Either use this column to help you think of your own details, or cover it up until you finish. (Share your results.)

Example: The jeep ride into the mountains (was rough.) _____   *scrambled my stomach*

1. (An empty cabin) served as our shelter. _____   *A cabin full of echoes*

2. Because it had been empty, it (had a strange smell.) _____   *smelled sour*

3. The windows were (covered with a dull film.) _____   *grown over with grime*

4. The wind began to (blow loudly.) _____   *howl*

5. Trees (rubbed against) the side of the cabin. _____   *scratched*

6. (A cold night air) moved in as the storm left. _____   *A frigid front*

7. (An amazing quiet) followed the storm. _____   *A penetrating calm*

8. A spring (softly poured) fresh, cool water. _____   *purred*

9. (A soft moss) covered the ground. _____   *Green velvet*

10. The view (was beautiful.) _____   *was breathtaking*

Sense Ability

▶ **Use sensory detail to write a "sense poem" about an object, an animal, or a person (possibly yourself). Use the following sense poem about ice cream as a model. You'll note that the details in lines 2-6 cover all of the senses.**

Line 1:	This
Line 2:	slurping, smacking *(sound)*
Line 3:	chunky, cocoa *(sight)*
Line 4:	slippery, cold *(touch)*
Line 5:	creamy, sweet *(taste)*
Line 6:	chocolaty, nutty *(smell)*
Line 7:	as a rocky road *("as" plus what it reminds you of)*
Line 8:	ice cream *(subject)*

Line 1: _____

Line 2: _____

Line 3: _____

Line 4: _____

Line 5: _____

Line 6: _____

Line 7: _____

Line 8: _____

FOLLOW-UP • Don't overlook the senses of smell, touch, and taste in your own writing. And don't be afraid to use your senses in creative ways. Tell your reader how a book tastes in a book report, how a baseball game smells in a descriptive story, and how a conversation feels in a personal experience paper.

SENTENCE-COMBINING WORKSHOPS

Improving Your Writing Style

Getting Started

Listen to this advice by writer Martyn Godfrey: "Don't be afraid to throw more than one verb in a sentence. I think *She twisted and fell* is more exciting than *She twisted. She fell to the ground.*" We happen to agree with Mr. Godfrey. *She twisted and fell* does sound more exciting, and reads more smoothly, than the two separate sentences. All of your favorite writers combine ideas just like this in their own work.

The **Sentence-Combining Workshops** in this section will help you learn about and practice this important technique. We have found that no other practice can do more to improve your writing style, so it is important that you put forth your best effort in these workshops. We also have included two workshops that deal with arranging and expanding sentences. You will look at sentence style in a whole new way in these last workshops.

Special Note: Your handbook contains a lot of good information related to sentence combining and sentence style. (Refer to "Sentence" in the index for this information.)

User's Checklist

Check your progress as you work on these **Sentence-Combining Workshops.**

☐ **Combining Sentences with Phrases** • *Calling all phrases!*

☐ **Combining Sentences with Adverb Clauses** • *There's a lot of weight in these words.*

☐ **Combining Sentences with Adjective Clauses** • *Moderation is always best.*

☐ **Sentence-Combining Review** • *Give me two "R's" a day.*

☐ **Meaningful Parts in a Sentence** • *Nonsense!*

☐ **Sentence Expanding** • *Letting Loose*

FOLLOW-UP • The best way to improve your style is to write often, experimenting with a number of different forms and techniques. (Refer to the list of exercises at the end of the "Styling Sentences" chapter in your handbook for some creative ideas.)

COMBINING SENTENCES WITH PHRASES

START-UP • Readers generally expect a certain amount of substance and rhythm as the ideas unfold in a piece of writing. Their expectations aren't met if the work is full of short, choppy sentences. That's why sentence-combining exercises can be so helpful. They give you practice producing sentences with enough body and form to keep readers interested in your ideas.

When it comes to sentence combining, the following types of phrases are often the key: **prepositional, participial, infinitive,** and **appositive phrases**. (Refer to "Phrase, Combining with" in the handbook index for explanations and examples.)

Calling all phrases!

► **Combine each pair of short sentences using the phrases indicated in parentheses. (Share your results.)**

1. I returned the stale Gummi Bears candy.
   It had been purchased at Ralph's Candy Shack. *(participial phrase)*

   _____

   _____

2. We rode in the stretch limousine.
   It was the one with the gold-plated wheel covers. *(prepositional phrase)*

   _____

   _____

3. Jerome's idea doesn't surprise me at all.
   His idea is to run full speed into the ice-cold water. *(infinitive phrase)*

   _____

   _____

4. My neighbor took me for a short flight in his private plane.
   He is a commercial pilot. *(appositive phrase)*

   _____

   _____

5. My older brother already left.
   He left for his first steel guitar lesson. *(prepositional phrase)*

   _____

   _____

6. The plot was discovered and stopped.
   The plot was to "toilet paper" my friend's house. *(infinitive phrase)*

   _____

   _____

7. The chapter is the one on photosynthesis.
   It is the one to read carefully. *(infinitive phrase)*

   _____

   _____

8. My best friend opened the meeting.
   He was reciting the pledge of allegiance. *(participial phrase)*

   _____

   _____

9. Fill that small pot before I get started.
   Fill it with water and garbanzo beans. *(prepositional phrase)*

   _____

   _____

FOLLOW-UP • Spend 3 to 5 minutes writing about what you eat when you are really, really hungry. Don't hold back. (If you exaggerate a little, no big deal.) As you review your writing, combine ideas as necessary to help your sentences read more effectively. Then exchange "menus" with a classmate.

COMBINING SENTENCES WITH ADVERB CLAUSES

START-UP • Words like *after, although, before,* and *unless* carry a lot of meaning. They tell you when, how, and under what conditions the main action of a sentence happens. These words are **subordinate conjunctions**, and they are used to form complex sentences.

The group of words introduced by the subordinate conjunction is called an **adverb clause**, and it can come at the beginning or at the end of a sentence. This all sounds more "complex" than it is. The best way to understand adverb clauses is to see some examples.

Chris made sure he had enough money. He ordered a pizza. (two sentences)

***Before he ordered a pizza**, Chris made sure he had enough money.* (Adverb clause at the beginning of a sentence—comma needed)

*Chris made sure he had enough money **before he ordered a pizza**.* (Adverb clause at the end of the sentence—no comma needed)

There's a lot of weight in these words.

▶ **Combine the following short sentences into one sentence using the subordinate conjunction given in parentheses. The first one is done for you.**

1. I was only four years old.
   I started kindergarten. *(when)*

   I was only four years old when I started kindergarten.

2. She checked her numbers. *(as)*
   The woman realized she held the winning lottery ticket.

   _____

   _____

   _____

3. I tried to stay calm.
   My heart was pounding. *(although)*

   _____

   _____

   _____

4. Kyna smiled innocently.
   She hadn't done anything wrong. *(as though)*

   _____

   _____

   _____

5. Bernadette felt lousy.
   She had lost her favorite necklace. *(because)*

   _____

   _____

   _____

6. Martin said he'd go to the party. *(after)*
   He had to ask his parents for their permission.

   _____

   _____

   _____

7. I winced.
   I saw the math exam. *(when)*

   _____

   _____

8. Mom left a note on the door.
   Dad would know where we went. *(so that)*

   _____

   _____

   _____

FOLLOW-UP • Write a paragraph or two about what happened this morning between the time you got up and the time you got to school. Try to put in as much detail as you can. Then exchange your writing with a classmate. Note ideas in one another's work that could be combined using adverb clauses.

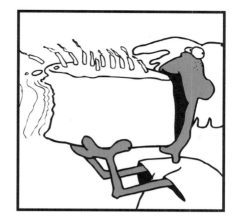

COMBINING SENTENCES WITH ADJECTIVE CLAUSES

START-UP • Writer and teacher Ken Macrorie warns young writers that heavy doses of "whos," "whiches," and "thats" in writing make it sound wordy, stiff, and impersonal. He advises moderation in the use of these words. (Their official name is **relative pronoun**.)

However, relative pronouns can be used effectively to help you combine ideas into complex sentences and avoid unnecessary repetition. (The part of a complex sentence beginning with *who, which,* or *that* is called an **adjective clause**.) Note the examples below.

Moderation is always best.

Example: The small bookstore could barely contain the **people**. The **people** came to meet Hank Aaron. (*People* is unnecessarily repeated in these sentences.)

Combined Sentence: The small bookstore could barely contain the people **who** came to meet Hank Aaron. (The repetition of *people* is avoided.)

Example: Hank Aaron was there signing his new **book** called "I Had a Hammer." The **book** had just been released. (*Book* is unnecessarily repeated.)

Combined Sentence: Hank Aaron was there signing his new book, **which** had just been released, called "I Had a Hammer." (The repetition of *book* is avoided.)

Special Challenge: Study the two combined sentences and determine why commas are used in the second sentence and not in the first one. State your theory on the following lines. (Share your theory with a classmate. Then compare it to the explanation in the handbook. See "Clause, Restrictive, nonrestrictive" in the index.)

_____

_____

_____

► **Combine each pair of sentences into one complex sentence using *who, which,* and *that* as connectors.** *Note:* **Key words and punctuation marks have already been put in place.**

1. My dad talked about buying Hank Aaron's new autobiography.
   My dad enjoys reading about sports figures.

   My dad, who _____ ,

   talked _____

   _____ .

2. Dad even brought along his prized possession—a baseball.
   The baseball had been signed by Eddie Matthews, a former teammate of
   Aaron's.

   Dad _____

   _____ baseball that _____

   _____ Aaron's.

3. There was already a line when we arrived at the bookstore.
   That line went all the way around the block.

   There _____

   _____ bookstore.

4. We were in line for almost two hours.
   Two hours is a long time when you're hungry and there's no hot-dog stand in
   sight!

   We _____ ,

   which _____

   _____ sight!

5. Hank Aaron signed books continually.
   Hank Aaron stayed an hour longer than scheduled.

   Hank Aaron, who _____ ,

   _____ continually.

6. My dad was very disappointed.
   My dad never did get Hank Aaron's autograph.

   _____ , who _____ ,

   _____ disappointed.

FOLLOW-UP • Conduct an informal study to see how personal or impersonal a particular textbook, newspaper, or magazine is. To proceed, circle or list all of the "whos,"
"whiches," and "thats" you can find on one page. (Select a page that contains more
words than pictures!) A heavy dose of relative pronouns suggests the material is
"textbookish," stiff, and formal in style.

SENTENCE-COMBINING REVIEW

START-UP • Two important practices should be established before sentence combining can have a significant effect on your writing. These practices are *writing* and *reading* on a regular basis (as in every day). Once you commit yourself to these two "R's," sentence combining and many other writing activities can make a difference in the way you compose.

Give me two "R's" a day.

▶ **Combine each set of simple sentences into longer, smoother-reading ones. (Make use of all of the combining techniques you have previously worked on. Also refer to "Sentence, Combining" in the handbook index for help.)**

1. Earl's father is taking a leave of absence.
   He has taught for 15 years.
   He teaches in a college.
   He will be writing a book.

   Earl's father, who has taught for 15 years in a college, is _____

   _____

2. The books were scattered.
   The books were for a science report.
   Magazines were scattered.
   The magazines were for personal reading.
   The books and magazines were scattered on Kim's desk.

   _____

   _____

   _____

3. The cafeteria was filled with laughter.
   The laughter was from students.
   The students were telling jokes.
   They were telling jokes about teachers.

   _____

   _____

   _____

▶ **Combine the following sets of simple sentences and then, on your own paper, finish the story. (The first combined sentence has been done for you.)**

Fernando found the right kind of film. The film was for his 35-mm camera.

Fernando found the right kind of film for his 35-mm camera.

He walked toward the checkout counter.
He noticed a poorly dressed man.
The man was standing next to a rack of watches.

_____

_____

The man skillfully put some of the watches in his coat pocket.
The man put them in his pocket quickly, too.

_____

_____

Fernando saw him do this. He didn't know what to do.

_____

_____

The man obviously was trying to shoplift merchandise.
He looked like he was really down on his luck.

_____

_____

Fernando moved toward the checkout counter.
A security guard came in sight.

_____

_____

Fernando . . . (Finish the story on your own paper.)

FOLLOW-UP • Exchange stories with a classmate. Find out how your partner developed the unfolding plot. Also note how effectively your partner combined ideas in his or her story.

MEANINGFUL PARTS IN A SENTENCE

START-UP • If someone asked you to *oblay* this *ointjay* or *oovgray* to some *oontays*, would you know how to respond? Probably not. As speakers and writers of English, we know that the italicized words aren't real. Our language sense tells us so. They are, in fact, examples of a twisted form of English called pig latin.

Students in the past have had fun playing with this altered form of English. Pig latin is formed by taking phrases like "blow this joint" or "groove to some tunes" and turning them inside out, so to speak. Try it yourself. Or, better yet, make up your own specialized language.

Scrambled Sentences

Our language alarm system can detect sentences that have been tampered with just as easily as it can detect bogus words. If someone said, "Clumsy plays Jack a tuba looking," our response would be, "Say what?" (or something along those lines). We know that sentences should clearly show someone doing something, as in "Jack plays a clumsy-looking tuba."

Nonsense!

▶ **In the following activity, you'll be asked to arrange the scrambled parts of sentences so they express thoughts that make good sense. Make sure to add the necessary capital letters and punctuation marks. (The starred word groups should be at the beginning of each of your unscrambled sentences.)**

Example: 1. slipping back to their holes
2. a couple of night crawlers
3. we spotted*

We spotted a couple of night crawlers slipping back to their holes.

1. with my sister and me
2. and turned on the TV
3. I went into the living room
4. sensing my mom was a little angry*

Sensing my mom was a little angry with my sister and me,

1. a horror movie
2. it gave me*
3. alone in my room

4. with the light off
5. the feeling of watching

_____

_____

_____

1. out for drama
2. I no longer
3. with boys on campus*

4. for the male roles
5. when I went
6. got recruited

— from *Me Me Me Me Me* by M. E. Kerr

_____

_____

_____

1. to the cows
2. hanging their lanterns*
3. my uncle and my cousins

4. from convenient pegs
5. and distributed the morning feedings
6. took hayforks

— from *Rascal* by Sterling North

_____

_____

_____

AFTER • THOUGHT Make sure you compare your results with the results of one or more of your classmates. There might be more than one way to organize the parts into effective sentences.

FOLLOW-UP • Find three or more smooth-reading or eye-opening sentences in a favorite book or magazine. Then scramble the important parts in each of these sentences. Exchange work and arrange your classmate's lists of parts into meaningful sentences. Compare your creations with the originals.

Note: Don't pick sentences that are unnecessarily long and confusing. The object of this activity is to help your partner see firsthand how effective sentences are put together, not to frustrate him or her.

SENTENCE EXPANDING

START-UP • What keeps us turning the pages of a good book, glued to our seats during an exciting movie, all eyes and ears during a heartwarming television show? We appreciate a good story. We're interested. And yes, we're all a little bit nosey. Writers are well aware of this and go to great effort to make sure that they satisfy our need to know by working plenty of detail into their stories.

Letting Loose

Details often spill out of the writer's mind spontaneously, naturally, as his or her writing develops. In this activity, you're going to be asked to "let loose" with some details in the same way that professional writers do. The result will be some interesting, expanded thoughts. (An example expanded sentence follows.)

Let's start with the following basic sentence:

> *Julie was studying.*

How could we let loose and expand this basic sentence?

- ■ First, we could say **when** she was studying:

> *Late last night Julie was studying.*

- ■ Second, we could say **where** she was studying:

> *Late last night Julie was studying at the kitchen table.*

- ■ Third, we could say **how** she was studying:

> *Late last night Julie was studying at the kitchen table, memorizing a list of vocabulary words.*

- ■ Finally, we could say **why** she was studying:

> *Late last night Julie was studying at the kitchen table, memorizing a list of vocabulary words for tomorrow's science quiz.*

Special Note: We could possibly add more information, but the sentence as it now stands reads well. The point is to make a smooth-reading, interesting sentence, not a sentence that is piled too high with detail. (See "Cumulative sentence" in the handbook index for more information on expanded sentences.)

▶ **Now you try. Expand the following brief thoughts with details where they naturally seem to fit—before, within, or after the basic sentence. (We'll help you with the first one below. Do the other four on your own paper.)**

    1. Roy slipped.
    2. Ms. Rogers entered.
    3. Jose swung.
    4. Marcia turned.
    5. The storm started.

The Writer's Corner

    Here are five types of detail you can use to expand basic ideas:

individual words: *quietly*
prepositional phrases: *at the kitchen table*
participial (-ing or -ed) **phrases:** *memorizing a list of words*
who, which, or *that* **clauses:** *who needed an A*
subordinate clauses: *because the semester was almost over*

How could you let loose and expand the first basic sentence? (Roy slipped.)

■ First, you could say **when** he slipped.

■ Second, you could say **where** he slipped.

■ Third, you could say **how** he slipped.

■ Fourth, you could say **why** he slipped. *(This fourth element is optional. If your sentence already says enough, leave it alone.)*

FOLLOW-UP • For more practice, write five of your own basic sentences. Then exchange them with a classmate and produce interesting expanded sentences from your partner's list. (Compare your work with your classmate's. Make note of sentences you especially like in each other's work.)

EDITING WORKSHOPS

Checking for Sentence and Usage Errors

You can accomplish a lot as a writer by following one basic rule: *Use clear and complete sentences.* Good writing, writing that effectively communicates an idea, is built on a foundation of clear and complete thoughts.

Your mind is already tuned in to sentences. You read sentences, hear sentences, and even think sentences. And for the most part, you use effective sentences when you develop your writing. But every writer—including your favorite authors—may occasionally make mistakes. That is why it is so important to check your work for sentence errors before you write a final draft.

As you probably know, our language is full of homophones, words that are pronounced alike but are different in meaning or spelling. Words like *their, there,* and *they're* are homophones. Using words like these correctly can be a real challenge. That is why it is also important to check your writing for usage errors.

The first set of **Editing Workshops** in this section will help you learn about or review common sentence errors. The second set of workshops deals with common usage errors. By completing the work in this section, you will become better able to identify and correct these types of errors in your writing.

Getting Started

User's Checklist

Check your progress as you work on these **Editing Workshops.**

☐ **Sentence Fragments** • *"Pacific" Facts*

☐ **Correcting Comma Splices and Run-Ons** • *A "Splice" of Summer Life*

☐ **Eliminating Wordiness** • *That's a mouthful!*

☐ **Adding Variety to Your Sentences** • *Time for a change?*

☐ **Avoid Rambling Sentences** • *. . . and they kept piling up!*

☐ **Using the Right Word 1** • *Locker cleanup?*

☐ **Using the Right Word 2** • *It's about time.*

☐ **Using the Right Word 3** • *Scavenger Hunt on Elm Street*

☐ **Using the Right Word—Review** • *Hit the road, Jack!*

FOLLOW-UP • Before you turn in a writing assignment, always have a trusted friend, classmate, or family member check your work for sentence and usage errors. All professional writers have editors who do the same. Why should you be any different?

SENTENCE FRAGMENTS

START-UP • A sentence fragment may look and sound like a sentence, but it isn't. Instead, it is a group of words that is missing either a subject or a verb or that doesn't express a complete thought. (Refer to "Fragment sentence" in the handbook index for examples of this sentence error.)

"Pacific" Facts

Some of the following groups of words are sentences, and some are not. Write an *S* on the line if it's a sentence; write an *F* if it's a fragment. Correct each word group labeled as a fragment.

Examples:

_____ S _____ The oceans are great bodies of water that cover more than 70 percent of the world's surface.

_____ F _____ *Oceans are also* ~~Also~~ commonly referred to as seas.

_____   1. Oceans maintain the earth's climate by regulating air temperature.

_____   2. Supplying moisture for rain.

_____   3. The Pacific Ocean, by far the largest individual ocean.

_____   4. The Pacific covers nearly a third of the earth's surface and could hold all the continents.

_____   5. It is also the deepest ocean, with an average depth of 12,900 feet.

_____   6. Every natural element found in the water of the oceans.

_____   7. Evaporation which removes freshwater from the oceans, leaving the salt behind.

_____   8. Rain returns freshwater to the oceans.

_____   9. The waters of the oceans move constantly.

_____ 10. Currents coursing through the seas like giant rivers.

▶ **Sentence fragments generally ride on the coattails of complete sentences. This means that fragments may often be corrected by joining them to either preceding or following sentences. In this activity, put an *S* above each sentence and an *F* above each fragment. Correct each fragment by joining it to the complete sentence or by adding what it needs to be a sentence on its own. The first one has been done for you.**

1. New York is one of the oldest states. A long, interesting history.
   S ..... F

   New York is one of the oldest states, so it has a long, interesting history.

2. Large groups of Indians lived there before white settlers arrived. Including the Algonquians and the Iroquois.

   _____

   _____

3. In the year 1624. The Dutch West India Company sent 30 families to settle New York.

   _____

   _____

4. What is now Manhattan used to be called New Amsterdam. Settled originally by the Dutch.

   _____

   _____

5. During the Revolutionary War. More than 30,000 people loyal to the British left New York.

   _____

   _____

6. New York was the 11th state to enter the Union after the war. Albany, the capital city, in the center of the state.

   _____

   _____

FOLLOW-UP • Exchange your work on sentence fragments with a classmate. Discuss any differences in each other's answers.

CORRECTING COMMA SPLICES AND RUN-ONS

START-UP • A **comma splice** is an error made when a writer connects two simple sentences with only a comma.

A **run-on sentence** occurs when two simple sentences run together without any punctuation marks and/or connecting words.

Example: *The day was going to be very hot, I like it that way.*

Discussion: Does this example contain one or two complete thoughts? There are two complete thoughts, but they are "spliced" together with only a comma (a comma splice). The easiest way to correct this sentence error is to add a coordinating conjunction (but) and turn it into a compound sentence.

Corrected Sentence: *The day was going to be very hot, but I like it that way.*

Example: *The summer day was to be the hottest of the year we decided to get up early.*

Discussion: Does this example contain one or two complete thoughts? Again, there are two complete thoughts, but they incorrectly run together (a run-on sentence). One way to correct this sentence error is to turn it into two separate sentences.

Corrected Sentence: *The summer day was to be the hottest of the year. We decided to get up early.*

A "Splice" of Summer Life

Place a CS in front of each comma splice, an RO in front of each run-on sentence, and a C in front of each correct sentence. Then correct each faulty sentence. (Refer to "Comma, Splice" and "Run-on sentence" in your handbook index for more information and examples.)

_____ 1. The forecast sounded a warning of very high temperatures.

_____ 2. Still, it looked like a great day for swimming, we headed for the beach.

_____ 3. By noon the heat was intense we needed to come in out of the sun.

_____ 4. It was the perfect time to go for a ride in the air-conditioned car, we decided to look for an ice-cream stand.

_____ 5. My mother loves the cooler temperatures air-conditioning produces.

_____ 6. The searing afternoon sun seemed ready to scorch everything in sight, we had come prepared with three bottles of sunscreen.

_____ 7. I didn't want to get a sunburn I remember the pain experienced the last time it happened.

_____ 8. We all brought along our beach hats the cool breeze from the water also kept us from overheating.

_____ 9. We had played it smart, and we were very happy about that fact.

_____ 10. It is sure to be hot again I think that these days are the most memorable.

_____ 11. I never complain about the weather, I just enjoy it.

_____ 12. After all, we can't change the weather.

FOLLOW-UP • Design a concrete poem for *comma splice* or *run-on sentence*. Use the space below for your finished product. (Refer to "Poetry, Invented" in the index for an example of concrete poetry as well as other poetry forms and ideas. Concrete poems might not be for everyone.)

ELIMINATING WORDINESS

START-UP • Resist the temptation to "pad" your writing with words and phrases that add nothing to the point you are trying to make. Also avoid "flowery" expressions, which sometimes sound good but seldom add anything worthwhile. (Refer to "Wordy sentence" in your handbook index for more information.)

That's a mouthful!

Make the following sentences clearer by eliminating any unnecessary words or phrases. Draw a line through these extra words or phrases. (Caution: Read these sentences very carefully. Some will sound fine at first even though they repeat ideas unnecessarily.)

Example: The former tenant ~~who had lived in the apartment before we moved in~~ painted all the walls ~~with a coat of~~ pink ~~paint~~.

1. As a general rule, most of the new submarines that were just purchased are atomic powered.

2. The canceled flight has been rescheduled for 5:15 p.m. tomorrow evening.

3. He arrived there in Terra Haute yesterday morning at 7:00 a.m. and gave a humorous speech that was very funny.

4. The very fast race car lapped all of the other cars that were in the race and made it look as if it were easy to do.

5. There are five people who want to drive in their cars to Sarah's house after the movie is over.

6. The difficult math problem, which was not easy to understand, caused me to fail the math test with an *F*.

7. The crowded shopping mall, which was filled to the brim with people, was evacuated at exactly 8:15 p.m. sharp.

8. The detective failed to solve the case because he didn't look for clues or spend time studying things at the scene of the crime.

9. He usually spends about two hours of his time each day working at his computer.

10. Despite the efforts of our team to defeat the opponent and win the game, they came up short and lost.

11. My brother he is taking bowling lessons at the bowling alley while my sister she is practicing her gymnastic routines. *(See "Subject, Double" in the handbook index for help.)*

12. In September my favorite rock group will return again here to repeat their recent performance at Center Stadium.

13. The final ending of the movie caught me by surprise because I didn't expect it.

14. After we had finished the chores that we worked on, my sister and I rushed in a hurry to the theater to see the main feature.

15. The road between Burlington and Elkhorn follows and bends along the winding White River, a stream with many twists and turns.

FOLLOW-UP • Write freely and rapidly for 5 to 8 minutes about one of the following subjects (or a subject of your own choosing). Make every effort to write nonstop so that the ideas flow freely.

Staying at a friend's house	The prettiest place I've ever seen
A narrow escape from trouble	The best pet I ever had

Next, see how wordy your free writing is. Cross out every word or phrase that is not absolutely necessary. Also have a classmate check your paper for wordy passages.

Special Challenge: Write a second draft of your paper—this time eliminating all unnecessary words and phrases. Share the results with the classmate who reviewed your first writing. Continue writing and revising if you like how this piece is shaping up.

ADDING VARIETY TO YOUR SENTENCES

START-UP • Use one-word modifiers, phrases, and clauses to add variety to your sentence beginnings. If too many of your sentences start the same way—with the subject—your writing may begin to sound dull or flat. (See "Variety of sentence structure" in your handbook index for more information.)

Time for a change?

Reword each of the following sentences twice. At the beginning of each of your sentences, use a word or word group other than the subject. Consider one-word modifiers, phrases, or clauses to start your revised sentences. (The subject in each sentence is highlighted in boldfaced type.)

1. Tempting **treasures** totaling billions of dollars lie waiting across the United States for treasure hunters.

   a. *Across the United States, tempting treasures totaling billions of dollars lie waiting for treasure hunters.*

   b. _____

   _____

2. Lost gold **mines** overgrown and hidden by time contain large fortunes in the western part of our country.

   a. _____

   _____

   b. _____

   _____

3. Famous **robbers** in fear for their lives often hid their plunder after holding up a bank or the stagecoach.

   a. _____

   _____

   b. _____

   _____

4. Many older **people**, distrustful of banks, at times stashed their valuables, which were never reclaimed.

   a. _____

   _____

   b. _____

   _____

5. Treasure **hunters** searching for a hot treasure prospect read old newspapers and magazines while the rest of us work regular jobs.

   a. _____

   _____

   b. _____

   _____

6. Old and interesting **objects**, in addition to gold, silver, and jewelry, are very valuable today because many people collect antiques.

   a. _____

   _____

   b. _____

   _____

7. A treasure hunter's most valuable **tool** surprisingly is his own mind, although a good metal detector can come in handy.

   a. _____

   _____

   b. _____

   _____

FOLLOW-UP • Read the opening two pages of "Styling Sentences" in your handbook. (See "Sentence, Styling" in your index.) Make note of two important things you learned about developing a sense of style. Share your findings with a classmate.

AVOID RAMBLING SENTENCES

START-UP • Just as you should correct any fragments, run-ons, or comma splices in your writing, you must also be careful not to use too many **and's** or **but's**. The result could well be a series of rambling sentences that could pile up.

... *and they kept piling up!*

▶ **Read the paragraphs below. Look and listen for sentences that ramble. Correct these sentences by taking out some (but not all) of the and's, but's, or so's. Then correct the capitalization and punctuation as necessary. (See "Rambling sentences" in your handbook index for help.)**

Our student council wanted to help families in need in our community, so we decided that we would have a canned-goods drive, but we needed to get students involved on a "massive" scale, and that is no small challenge.

Our advisor, Miss Daniels, thought of starting a friendly competition. Each of the homerooms would compete against the other homerooms, and one homeroom in each grade level would win not only recognition in the newspaper but also a pizza party, and that meant fame and fortune were awaiting the winning homerooms.

Mr. Brzinski's homeroom began the food drive by bringing in the first canned goods, and then Ms. Maher's homeroom got in the act, and before we knew it, all the homerooms were involved, and for the next two weeks, students were mowing lawns, baby-sitting, and buying canned goods, and adding to each homeroom's total. We announced the totals at the end of each day and stacked the cans on the stage in the gymnasium so everybody could see their homeroom's progress.

To say the least, we were more than pleased with the results, and the newspaper took pictures of the huge piles of cans, and we knew that we had helped many people, and that was the best reward of all.

USING THE RIGHT WORD 1

Locker cleanup?

START-UP • The series of activities that follow identify many of the pairs of words that are often misused.
Make special note of the words that "commonly" con-
fuse you. Also turn to "Using the Right Word" in your
handbook whenever you have a usage question. (See
"Usage and commonly mixed pairs" in the index.)

**If the underlined word is incorrect, cross out the word
and write the correct form above it. Do not change a
word that is correct.**

                              heard
Example: We had all ~~herd~~ the principal's voice
               through
               ~~threw~~ the PA system.

1. Their was no mistaking the announcement: "Students which have lockers in the
   upper hall will have locker cleanup this morning."

2. "I knew I should have done that last weak", I thought.

3. "Your in for it now," snickered our homeroom teacher.

4. Seeing our paned looks, teachers walked buy with words of encouragement.

5. "Don't leave those apples in their any longer," counciled one teacher.

6. Tami and Al, my too neighbors, had already cleaned there lockers, making it worse.

7. "Give him a wide berth there," said Mr. Gonzales. "He needs more room."

8. "I don't no how you can leave that locker get so messy," he continued.

9. But the last laugh was on Mr. G., four only too minutes after we got back too
   our homerooms, the vice-principle announced that all eighth-grade students
   should check to see if there teachers' desks needed to be cleaned as well!

10. Mr. G. wrote "Clean me" on his stationary, and we laughed altogether.

USING THE RIGHT WORD 2

START-UP • When is it important to know if one word (good) should be used instead of another word (well)? The answer to that is easy. It's important to use the right word whenever you are going to share your thoughts in a formal or semiformal situation. For example, whenever you write a report for a science class, speak in front of a church group, or write a letter requesting information, you should use the language correctly. An informed and educated public expects it.

It's about time.

If the underlined word is incorrect, cross out the word and write the correct form above it. Do not change a word that is correct.

Example: As part of our civics class, we formed a ~~counsel~~ *council* to decide on ~~witch~~ *which*

items to put in a time capsule.

1. We <u>knew</u> we had limited space in the capsule we had made, so we <u>choose</u> many

small items.

2. I <u>excepted</u> many ideas from the other members of the class, and that <u>lead</u> to

many interesting discussions.

3. The teacher said that we had to be <u>real</u> sure that we didn't put in things that

would <u>brake</u>.

4. We needed to seal the items in plastic and let out all the <u>heir</u>.

5. My dad told us the school <u>bored</u> would like to <u>here</u> about this project.

6. I had to <u>by</u> some film to take photographs <u>for</u> the newspaper.

7. We <u>through</u> in some bottle tops, baseball cards, and <u>some</u> of my mom's <u>personnel</u>

<u>stationery</u>.

8. As I held the capsule in my hand, I told everybody that the items <u>wood</u> be worth

<u>alot</u> in the future.

9. The council decided that the year 2041 wood be a good year too open the capsule.

10. Instructions kept in the school safe will direct the principle to open the capsule in front of the whole school.

11. We finally painted the capsule bright read and buried it behind a set of lockers between two walls.

12. The counsel maid a pact to visit the school on that "historic" day in 2041 and relive our passed.

FOLLOW-UP • With a partner or a group of classmates, discuss the possibility of creating your own time capsule. What are some *items* that represent your interests, your school, and your time in history? What will your capsule look like? Where will you place it? When would you want the capsule opened? Brainstorm for "time capsule" ideas below.

Items   The Capsule Design

_____ _____

_____ _____

_____ _____

_____ _____

_____ _____

The Plan:

USING THE RIGHT WORD 3

Scavenger Hunt on Elm Street

▶ **If the underlined word is incorrect, cross out the word and write the correct form above it. Do not change a word that is correct.**

Example: Since we've moved ~~two~~ *to* Elm Street,

our ~~perennial~~ *annual* scavenger hunts are

more fun ~~then~~ *than* ever.

1. Moving to Elm Street <u>seamed</u> to <u>infer</u> that

   <u>their</u> would be danger involved in our scavenger hunts.

2. My good friend Freddy—that's his real name—helped us <u>raze</u> money to <u>by</u>

   everything we needed.

3. Although four teams of eighth-grade friends <u>seemed</u> like a large <u>amount</u> of

   kids, we did manage to get them <u>altogether</u> on the evening of the hunt.

4. <u>Latter</u> that evening, when my mom <u>blue</u> the whistle, the games began.

5. Jim's team built a lead by getting half of the items on the list from <u>Ant</u>

   Mary's house, including a <u>pare</u> of glass paperweights.

6. My best friend Sam did <u>good</u> finding a stamp with a grizzly <u>bare</u> on it in a

   stack of <u>male</u> on the hall table.

7. Melissa's team found the <u>soul</u> of an old <u>blew</u> tennis shoe in the park.

8. It took my team <u>too</u> hours before it finally found a Boy Scout troop <u>metal</u>.

9. But it was Sam <u>which</u> won the contest by entering the <u>desserted</u> house near

   the river and getting the Freddie Krueger glove I <u>through</u> in <u>their</u> earlier.

10. We all <u>complemented</u> him on that <u>peace</u> of bravery.

USING THE RIGHT WORD—REVIEW

Hit the road, Jack!

> Correct any errors by drawing a line through the error and writing the correct form above. Do not change any word that is correct.

Example: When my dad was 15, he couldn't
~~weight~~ *wait* to have his dad ~~learn~~ *teach* him how
~~too~~ *to* drive.

1. My grandfather choose to tell me the tale last weak.

2. "Jack, its a good day for your first lesson," said Grandpa John.

3. After alot of reminders about the "rules of the road," my grandpa and dad were already to hit the road.

4. "Son, let's get some practice in before the whether turns rainy," said my grandfather on that fateful mourning.

5. It must have been scary for Dad, setting behind the wheel of Grandpa's new car.

6. With a chuckle Grandpa told me, "You're dad's knees probably felt weak."

7. He said that Dad needed alot of reminding about witch buttons and levers too push and when to push them.

8. Dad seamed nervous buy the time he was ready to pull out of the driveway, and he accidentally blue the horn.

9. Grandpa admitted their was some nervousness on his part, to.

10. He tried to compliment Dad on everything he did write as they safely past a slow-moving truck.

11. Of coarse, he choose to be positive with his son.

12. But Grandpa admitted to me, "Every time you're father came too a stop, I hit my own imaginary break."

13. Some miles farther down the road, Grandpa herd a gasp from the knew driver.

14. Dad maid a turn to soon and almost ran rite into a parked car.

15. "Its not going to be a good day," thought Grandpa.

16. "After that, I kept picturing my new car as a mangled mass of medal," admitted my grandfather.

17. "Well, Grandpa, at least you weren't board with the driving lesson," I said.

18. Grandpa chuckled. "On the contrary," he said, "I almost feinted that day."

19. Grandpa said that if nothing else, he taught Dad a very important principal of driving: Keep you're eyes on the road!

20. They're we were, both laughing, when Dad came out on the porch and sat besides me and asked what was up.

21. Grandpa smiled at me and said, "Jack, before you no it, you'll go threw it yourself with little Johnny hear."

22. The next mourning, Dad razed the question again about Grandpa's personnel comments.

23. "Its almost time four my first driving lesson," I replied casually.

24. Their was a sudden paned expression on his face.

Helpful Hint: Use the memory aid "The princi**pal** is my **pal**" to remember the difference between *principle* (a rule or truth) and *principal* (the person in charge of a school).

FOLLOW-UP • Using the right word in your writing is important, so try to get to know which is "witch" and which is "which." Become familiar with words that are commonly misused and make every effort to keep your writing correct and natural. Finally, whenever you have a question, refer to your handbook or favorite dictionary. They're user-friendly.

PROOFREADING WORKSHOPS

Using Capital Letters and Punctuation

Capital letters and punctuation marks are important parts of your language system. They help you keep your words and ideas under control while you write. And they help your readers enjoy the finished products you share with them. Capital letters and punctuation marks are the road markers that allow them to travel through your writing without getting lost.

While we automatically use these road markers during the writing process, we don't always use them correctly, or in the right places. That is why it is so important to proofread the final copy of your writing before you share it. You want all of the capital letters and punctuation marks to be in place, directing the flow of your ideas.

The seven **Proofreading Workshops** in this section provide a review of the common uses of capital letters and punctuation marks. As you complete your work, you will learn how helpful "The Yellow Pages" in the handbook can be when you proofread. (This section is easy to find because it is color-coded yellow.)

Getting Started

User's Checklist

Check your progress as you work on these **Proofreading Workshops**.

☐ **Reviewing Caps and Abbreviations** • *A Mexican Fiesta*

☐ **End Punctuation Review** • *Say cheese!*

☐ **Using Commas** • *"Comma comma do wha ditty . . ."*

☐ **Punctuating Dialogue** • *Sports Talk*

☐ **Using the Apostrophe** • *I'm a possessive person!*

☐ **Using Other Forms of Punctuation** • *Pizza Delivery Day*

☐ **Punctuation Review** • *What has eight arms, a soft body, . . .*

FOLLOW-UP • No one expects you to know *all* of the punctuation and capitalization rules. But everyone expects you to know and follow the basic rules of mechanics. Otherwise, your writing will be too hard to follow.

REVIEWING CAPS AND ABBREVIATIONS

START-UP • **Attention to detail** means different things depending on the task . . . but the result will always be the same: a better party, a smoother-running classroom, a tastier pie, and a finer piece of writing.

In this activity you will review a series of phrases or sentences to make sure that capital letters (and abbreviations) have properly been put in place. It's hard to keep track of all of the rules, especially if you haven't reviewed them in a long time, so make good use of the rules listed in your handbook. (Refer to "Capitalization" and "Abbreviations" in the index.)

A Mexican Fiesta

Put a line through any word or letter below that is capitalized or abbreviated incorrectly. Correct each error.

An activity strategy: Go through the list once and make the changes you're sure of. Then, for those which you question, review the rules in your handbook. Still stuck? Ask a classmate. And if all else fails, ask your teacher!

Example: We were looking for a project for our ~~s~~pringfield ~~m~~iddle ~~s~~chool ~~g~~lobal ~~s~~tudies ~~f~~air for ~~j~~anuary.

1. How about a fiesta highlighting mexican culture?

2. what a great idea for the middle of Winter!

3. mr. brown, our Global Studies teacher, is asking us to put together a fiesta, or party.

4. our class, global studies 101, will bring the food.

5. mr. brown says that other classes will be responsible for planning the schedule of events by this Wed.

6. May we get parents involved from the springfield parent teacher assoc.?

7. Yes, we need a lot of help and maybe a few $'s, too.

8. The fiesta will involve spanish music and a few festival customs from Mex.

9. mr. whitman, the gym teacher, will teach all of the eighth graders the mexican hat dance.

10. in the art 101 classes, all of the students will make posters and wall decorations.

11. The springfield middle school band will perform all of the music for the fiesta.

12. the band director, mr. ames, has written a special party song, and he tells us it's called "the old brown dog."

13. We can't wait to hear his song written for jazz, his dog.

14. He's a very creative person, and he sings like sting.

15. My chorus 102 class will sing backup with miss thompson.

16. we're calling the event springfield's fiesta fantastic.

17. The South end of the gym is reserved for the Pinata bashing.

18. Springfield's fiesta Fantastic is scheduled for jan 30.

19. the *Springfield daily Trib.* will come and take pictures.

20. what a great way to study the spanish-mexican cultures!

FOLLOW-UP • Think of an incident where you and a teacher have been in "the same boat together." This could be something fun like planning an assembly program, an end-of-the-year cleanup, or something as serious as a tornado, an earthquake, or a fire drill. Write a paragraph or two about this experience. Exchange finished products with a partner and discuss each other's work.

END PUNCTUATION REVIEW

START-UP • Punctuation, along with capitalization, controls the movement of your writing. The end punctuation marks—periods, question marks, exclamation points—signal the end of a sentence. Commas signal the breaks or pauses in a sentence. Considering these two simple points, punctuation—especially end punctuation—is not a difficult part of writing.

Say cheese!

▶ **Place periods, question marks, and exclamation points where they are needed in the following narrative. Also supply the necessary capital letters. (Refer to "Punctuation, marking" in your handbook index for rules and examples.)**

Example: I had applied for a position on the yearbook staff during the first week of school. What a thrill to find out I made it! Was I going to be able to do a good job? I would find out on group picture day.

my friends and i were very excited that it was finally group picture

day carrie, kim, and i were responsible for making sure that everybody

who was in a group got his or her picture taken what a difficult job

how could we be sure that everybody would be in the right place at the

right time were we up to this task we were about to find out

we decided that the teachers themselves should make sure that all

of their activity members were at the right place at the right time for

the pictures we told the teachers to check off the students' names as they arrived for the picture we provided the checklist what a great idea I'd like to take credit for the checklist unfortunately, I can't it was carrie's brainstorm

we also made sure that announcements were made at regular intervals so students were constantly reminded of the picture schedule ahead of time one announcement read, for example, " please have students from student council report to the multipurpose room " the announcements were my responsibility

we scheduled all groups during the morning periods when no students had gym would you want your picture taken in a "geeky" gym suit what a fantastic system do it right and it will go right

i'm happy that nothing went wrong as a matter of fact, everything went very well the only thing the students had to do to get in the yearbook was listen for the announcements of their activities and get checked off by their advisors of course, they also had to say, " cheeeeeese "

FOLLOW-UP • Write a journal entry (or a first draft) about an experience in your life that first worried you but, when it finally arrived, turned out to be no problem at all. Organize your thoughts in chronological order and try to use transition words (*next, finally,* etc.). Don't forget to "spice up" your writing with all four of the different types of sentences: *commands, statements, exclamations,* and *questions.*

USING COMMAS

START-UP • Of all of the punctuation marks, the one that has the most uses (and probably causes the most confusion) is the comma. You will note that your handbook devotes 15 topic numbers to the different rules for using commas. Do we (the handbook editors and your teachers) expect you to memorize all of these rules? No . . . but we would like you to become familiar with as many of them as you can. That's why we've designed this activity. Read on and become better acquainted with commas.

"Comma comma do wha ditty . . ."

▶ **Review the comma rules in your handbook and then fill in the blanks below. Place commas correctly in each sample sentence.**

1. Commas are used between words, _____, or clauses in a series that

   contains at least _____ items.

   I love to spend time at amusement parks the movies and concerts.

2. Commas are used to distinguish hundreds, _____, millions, etc., in

   _____.

   There were 4 0 0 0 0 people at the last concert I attended.

3. Commas are used in addresses and _____ to make them more clear.

   We ordered our tickets from Ticketmaster Sales 4004 West Main Street

   Chicago Illinois 60110. The tickets should arrive by May 5 1994.

4. Commas are used to set off the exact _____ of the speaker _____
   the rest of the sentence.

   "I'm sure " said Dad "that you can take some friends to the concert."

5. Commas are used to separate an interjection or _____ _____
   from the rest of the sentence.

   No we don't want to sit in the back rows of the stadium.

6. Commas are used to set off an _____ of the main thought of a sentence.

   The front row if you asked me would be the best place to sit.

7. A comma may be used between two _____ clauses that are joined

   by _____ conjunctions.

   We were going to take the van but the old thing wouldn't start.

8. Commas are used to enclose a _____ , name, or initials which follow a

   person's last _____ .

   Our tickets came addressed to Adams J. T. Johns T. G. and Kendall M. A.

9. Commas are used to _____ two or more _____ that
   equally modify the same noun.

   We beamed with joy as we held the expensive long-awaited tickets.

10. A comma should separate an _____ clause or a long modifying

    _____ from the independent clause that follows it.

    After many months passed the day of the concert arrived.

    While we had waited another act had been added to the show.

11. Comma _____ can be avoided by adding a _____
    after the comma when hooking up two independent clauses.

    Outside concerts are not my favorite type, _____ (insert conjunction)

    they can be fun in warm weather.

12. Commas should separate an _____ phrase (or appositive) from
    the rest of the sentence.

    My dad an expert concertgoer was a big help in our planning.

13. Use a comma to separate a _____ of direct _____ from the rest
    of the sentence.

    Dad check out this excellent forecast—no rain!

14. Commas are used to punctuate _____ phrases and clauses

    (those that are not _____ to the basic meaning of the sentence).

    Jim and Chris both wearing hats were eager to get into the concert.

15. Commas should ***not*** be placed around _____ phrases and clauses

   (those that are needed for the clear _____ of the sentence).

   *The color-coded tickets indicated that we had to sit in the seats **that were painted orange.***

   (The final clause contains important information. Therefore, it is not set off from the rest of the sentence with a comma.)

Practice Using Commas

After reviewing the comma rules in the previous exercise, place commas correctly in the following sentences.

1. Dad here are the good seats we've been telling you about.

2. "Wow " said Chris "these are great!"

3. The usher a young man with a beard heard him and smiled.

4. Dad took snack-bar orders and went to get sodas popcorn and pretzels.

5. The attendance by the way turned out to be over 42 000.

6. The names and locations of Caroline Adams M.D. and Samuel Cline M.D. were posted on signs near the stage in case of emergencies.

7. We were surprised to see Miss Daniels our English teacher at the concert.

8. I looked at my ticket dated August 10 1994.

9. The music which sounded perfect from our seats carried out to the far expansive reaches of the stadium.

10. The concert was fantastic, _____ (insert conjunction) the weather was perfect.

FOLLOW-UP • Come up with three sentences to describe an event you've attended. (For fun, try making the sentences confusing before the commas are added.) Share your work with a friend.

Example: *While watching the lead singer jump my brother dropped his pretzel.*
(A comma is definitely needed after "jump.")

PUNCTUATING DIALOGUE

START-UP • You don't even have to think about talking . . . it just happens. But putting "talking" into writing is a bit different. There are a number of rules to follow when using quotation marks, commas, end marks, and capital letters. This activity will give you a chance to review those rules and put them to good use.

Sports Talk

▶ **Punctuate the following sentences with quotation marks, commas, and end marks. Make sure to review the rules in your handbook for punctuating dialogue before you work on these sentences.**

Note: In a broken quotation, the dialogue, or "talk," is interrupted by references to the speaker (Jerome said, replied Sonia). Punctuate broken quotations in the following ways:

"The play's on second," called Naomi. *"Throw the ball."*
(A period is placed after "Naomi" to signal the end of one sentence.)

"We've got them now," said Corey, *"and all we need is one more out."*
(A comma is placed after "Corey" because the sentence of dialogue
does not end after the interruption.)

1. I'm pitching said Jamie before they tie this game up

2. I gave it my best exclaimed Yvonne but my arm's sore

3. Jamie heard the pained voice and said Yvonne, don't worry about it

4. Let's play ball came the call from the ump

5. Terri and Andrea yelled Come on, Jamie, we need one more out

6. Jamie delivered the ball, and after the routine force play was made,

   Yvonne approached the mound and said Thanks, Jamie, for understanding

7. No problem said Jamie We're a team and don't forget it

8. Yvonne said You're a good friend and a very good relief pitcher

FOLLOW-UP • Re-create a phone conversation (or make one up) between you and a friend or parent or . . . Make the conversation as realistic as possible. (Check the punctuation carefully before you share the finished product with your classmates.)

USING THE APOSTROPHE

START-UP • An apostrophe has several very important uses. It is used to show that letters have been left out of words (don't), to show possession (Garfield's dinner), and to indicate time or amount (a day's work).

Review the rules in your handbook about using apostrophes. (Refer to "Possessives, forming" in the index.) Then complete the following statements.

Singular Possessive: The possessive form of singular nouns is usually made by adding

_____ .

Plural Possessive: The possessive form of plural nouns ending in *s* is usually made by

adding _____ .

For plural nouns not ending in *s*, _____ must be added.

I'm a possessive person!

Punctuate the following sentences correctly, using apostrophes as necessary. Be sure to cross out the word in question and write the correct answer above it to avoid confusion.

Example: "~~Didnt~~ *Didn't* your ~~sisters~~ *sister's* puppy chew up ~~yesterdays~~ *yesterday's* homework,

Homer?"

1. "Ill get to tomorrows assignments after this television show," I called.

2. My moms quick answer was, "No you wont. Youll work on them right

   now."

3. Mr. Basss homework wasnt too hard. It was the physics I couldnt face.

4. Besides that, when the seasons new shows are on, its hard to do work.

5. "Cant I take a break, Mom?" I pleaded as though my entire familys sanity

   were at stake.

6. "Youve been on break!" was my moms reply.

7. I shouldve finished in study hall, but instead I had helped Mr. Anderson with his bulletin board entitled "The Class of 99 in the Workplace."

8. Im learning that when students homework isnt done, it comes back to haunt them; so I started to work.

9. The evenings fears of Ds and Fs in my classes vanished in the next 30 minutes, and the next days homework was completed.

10. My advice: Get your homework done as soon as you can or itll be tomorrows nightmare!

FOLLOW-UP • Review the rules for possessives in your handbook and then add apostrophes as needed in the following phrases:

❑ Fuddle, Muddle, and Bamboozles magic act

❑ Leonardos, Raphaels, and Michelangelos pizzas

❑ my brother-in-laws yo-yo

❑ their sisters-in-laws roller skates

❑ everybodys pet rock

❑ yesterdays fads

USING OTHER FORMS OF PUNCTUATION

START-UP • If you look at the chart of punctuation marks in your handbook, you'll see that there are many marks available to you. You'll find these marks very valuable, especially as the thoughts you express in writing become more complex. Some of the important punctuation marks in this list include **semicolons [;]**, **colons [:]**, **dashes [—]**, **hyphens [-]**, **parentheses [()]**, and the **ellipsis [. . .]**.

Pizza Delivery Day

▶ **Review the punctuation rules in your handbook and then fill in the blanks below. Place punctuation marks correctly in each sample sentence.**

1. Semicolons are used to join two _____ _____ , or sentences, not connected with a coordinate conjunction.

   We raised money for our outdoor education program by selling pizzas

   and sausages delivery day is today.

2. A colon is used to introduce a _____ , _____ , or important point.

   To earn money we sold the following cheese pizzas, sausage pizzas,

   pepperoni pizzas, cutters, and sausages.

3. A dash can be used to indicate a _____ _____

   in a sentence, to emphasize a word(s), a phrase, or a _____ , and

   to show that someone's speech is being _____ .

   The pizza order forms I hope I added mine up correctly were handed

   in to Mr. Pennington.

4. A hyphen can be used to create _____ words beginning with

   the prefixes _____ , _____ , _____ , and "great."

   After delivering hundreds of pizzas, I knew I'd want to become an

   ex salesperson.

5. Parentheses are used around words included in a sentence to _____ information or to help make an _____ clearer.

   The pizza order forms included a lot of information addresses, phone numbers, prices, customer totals that helped make the deliveries easy.

6. An ellipsis may be used to show a pause or an _____ of words.

   "You need your pizzas by 5:00? Well, I ah okay, I'll be there."

▶ **Punctuate the following sentences correctly by adding the necessary colons, semicolons, dashes, hyphens, parentheses, and ellipses. (The first one is done for you.)**

1. The semitruck pulled up, and we were ready for the 299 cases of pizzas; we all jumped to our stations.

2. We needed fifteen students to process the delivery system and five to give the parents some valuable information where to park. *(for emphasis)*

3. Each step of the system sign-in, pickup, loading, and carryout had to run like clockwork. *(added information)*

4. The driver had separated all of the items cheese pizzas, sausage pizzas, pepperoni pizzas, pizza cutters, and sausages.

5. Safety is one thing that is very important actually vital in the car-loading station. *(sudden break)*

6. Mr. Pennington inspected the whole operation, but we all worked to make it an accident free day. *(creating a new word)*

7. The sale was a success we had handled 145 orders and 3,578 pizzas!

8. Mr. Pennington was pleased. "I just want you to know that we've earned approximately four no make that five thousand dollars!" *(pause in dialogue)*

▶ **As you can see, these advanced uses of punctuation can make your writing more intelligible, more interesting, and more exciting. Try your hand at it in your own writing. Use the six forms of punctuation highlighted in this section.**

PUNCTUATION REVIEW

What has eight arms, a soft body, . . .

Proofread the paragraphs below. Draw a line through any mark of punctuation or capital letter that is used incorrectly. Add any needed punctuation or capital letters. Refer to your handbook for help.

An octopus is a Marine animal with eight arms called tentacles. It has a soft body large eyes and a strong jaw. The octopus uses its arms to catch clams crabs lobsters and other Shellfish for food. It cuts up its food with its horny jaws, which come to a point like a birds beak. Because of octopuses scary appearance some people call them devilfish; but octopuses rarely, if ever, attack people.

Most of the 50 different kinds of octopuses are actually about the size of a persons fist. There are larger ones however that measure 28 feet from the tip of one arm to the tip of another but even these octopuses are more likely to be eaten by humans than the other way around. Octopuses live chiefly in the china and mediterranean Seas, and many people in these Regions eat octopus meat.

The octopus in almost every respect is a one of a kind creature it has no bones and no shell. but it does have a highly developed brain an octopus also has three Hearts. It swims by drawing water into it's body and then squeezing it out in bursts through a funnel shaped opening under it's head. The force of the water propels the octopus backward the octopus can also squirt out Black fluid that forms a cloud around the animal, hiding it from it's enemies.

Octopuses really are a lot more interesting than your average Fish!

FOLLOW-UP • Compare your corrections with a classmate's. Discuss any differences and double-check points of confusion with your handbook.

PART III
Language and Learning Workshops

LANGUAGE WORKSHOPS

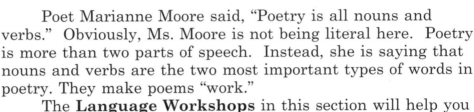

Making Words "Work" for You

Poet Marianne Moore said, "Poetry is all nouns and verbs." Obviously, Ms. Moore is not being literal here. Poetry is more than two parts of speech. Instead, she is saying that nouns and verbs are the two most important types of words in poetry. They make poems "work."

The **Language Workshops** in this section will help you make words work in your own writing. For example, in "Where'd he come from?" you'll learn about using vivid verbs. And in "It could only happen to me!" you'll learn about using colorful adjectives. Additional workshops review different parts of speech. (In one form or another, all eight parts of speech are addressed in this section.)

We have designed these workshops to help you in two different ways. First, we want you to understand and appreciate more fully the standard use of the language. By standard use, we mean the language you would use in a classroom setting. Second, we want you to be aware of the importance of word choice in your writing.

Special Note: "The Yellow Pages" in your handbook is your complete grammar, usage, and mechanics guide. Become familiar with this section. You will be asked to turn to it often in these workshops.

Getting Started

User's Checklist

Check your progress as you work on these **Language Workshops.**

☐ **Nouns in Review** • *"NounBank"*

☐ **Identifying Verbals** • *Secret Agents of Writing*

☐ **Using Vivid Verbs** • *Where'd he come from?*

☐ **Subject-Verb Agreement** • *Writing "Agreeable" Sentences*

☐ **Special Agreement Problems** • *Can't we agree on anything?*

☐ **Adverbs: A Quick Review** • *Sailing . . . Sailing away!*

☐ **Comparing with Adverbs** • *I'm positive. That's comparative.*

☐ **Identifying Double Negatives** • *This couldn't hardly be an adverb!*

☐ **Adjectives at Work** • *It could only happen to me!*

☐ **Using Adjectives to Compare** • *My cat's bigger than your cat.*

☐ **Reviewing Pronouns** • *Greasing Your Writing*

☐ **Pronoun Problems** • *That's indefinitely a challenge!*

☐ **Intensive and Reflexive Pronouns** • *Mirror, mirror, on the wall . . .*

☐ **Interjections and Prepositions** • *Oh no! It's another math test.*

☐ **Using Coordinate Conjunctions** • *Pleasing a Reader's Ear*

☐ **Parts of Speech Review** • *Eight is enough.*

FOLLOW-UP • Do you have to become an expert grammarian to become a good writer? No, but you do need a good working knowledge of the language. Your handbook is full of helpful information about using the language correctly and effectively. Refer to it often.

NOUNS IN REVIEW

"NounBank"

▶ In the space below, freely list common nouns as they come to mind. (They are the ones that don't begin with capital letters.) Test your common k(noun)ledge by filling in the space in 3 to 5 minutes.

Common K(noun)ledge

Get your "word's worth" in a poem.

▶ Write a title-down poem for one of the nouns in your list. (Refer to "Title-down poetry" in the handbook index for an example.)

FOLLOW-UP • On your own paper, explain what is meant by the following types of nouns: *proper nouns, concrete nouns, abstract nouns,* and *collective nouns.* (Don't look in your handbook.) Share your explanations with a classmate. Then compare your explanations with the ones in *Write Source 2000.*

IDENTIFYING VERBALS

Secret Agents of Writing

START-UP • Hidden in many pieces of writing are secret agents known as verbals. A **verbal** is a verb acting as another part of speech; it's a verb in disguise. **Gerunds**, **participles**, and **infinitives** are verbals.

A *gerund* is a verb form ending in *-ing* and is used as a noun.

> **Example:** *Shopping* is excellent recreation.
> (*Shopping* is the noun subject.)

A *participle* is a verb form ending in *-ed* or *-ing* and is used as an adjective.

> **Example:** The butterfly *fluttering* near the daisy is a monarch.
> (*Fluttering* modifies "butterfly.")

An *infinitive* is a verb form introduced by the word "to" and can be used as a noun, an adjective, or an adverb.

> **Example:** I plan *to read* a book on Saturday. (*To read* is a noun used as a direct object.)

▶ **In the following paragraph, verbals are underlined. Above each of these words, identify what kind of verbal it is—gerund, participle, or infinitive. (The first one is done for you.)**

participle

Idalia, bored with the usual birthday presents like socks, asked for a pet for her birthday this year. Walking a dog of her own had been Idalia's secret dream for a long time. A poodle puppy wagging its tail in the window of a pet store caught her eye in the mall. Hoping for this pet, Idalia went to the mall every day for two weeks to look at the beloved pup. When her birthday came, Idalia and her mom hurried to the store to buy the poodle. Idalia named the excited puppy Inglebert, meaning "unusually intelligent." Playing fetch and teaching Inglebert new tricks now take up much of Idalia's time.

FOLLOW-UP • On your own piece of paper, write a paragraph about an animal in your life. Use at least one example of each kind of verbal in your paragraph. Then exchange paragraphs with a classmate and circle the verbals in each other's work.

Special Challenge: Identify what kind of verbal each one is.

USING VIVID VERBS

Where'd he come from?

START-UP • A sentence like "The plane flew past Ralphy" is too general to create an effective image or word picture. A reader can't see *how* the plane was flying, or how close it flew to Ralphy, or *what* it sounded like.

On the other hand, if the sentence were to say "The plane screamed past Ralphy," the reader would be able to see things more clearly. A vivid verb like *scream* makes the sentence come alive for the reader. Vivid verbs add punch to writing. They make writing "scream" rather than "fly."

Verb Medley

► **Read the "Helpful Hint" printed in the section about vivid verbs in your handbook. (Refer to "Vivid details, Verbs" in the index.) Then fill in the blanks in the sentences that follow. (Make good use of this advice in your own writing.)**

Avoid using the _____ too often.

Many times a_____ can be made from

another word in the _____ .

► **In each of the sentences below, substitute one vivid verb for the verb and adverb in parentheses.**

Example: Brett _____*tore*_____ (quickly went) across the burning sand.

1. Donna_____ (carefully read) the tag on her parachute.

2. Kevin _____ (went quickly) past the sleeping Doberman.

3. Suzy _____ (moved quickly) past the other runners.

4. Miss Tinely _____ (spoke loudly) at her daydreaming friend.

5. Tim _____ (looked quickly) at the fuel gauge.

6. The white rhinoceros _____ (walked heavily) down the ramp.

7. The mice _____ (moved quickly) to their hiding places.

8. The writer _____ (looked blankly) at the unopened letter.

▶ **In the paragraph below, substitute a vivid verb for any verb in parentheses that you feel needs improving.** (*Note:* **Do not replace every verb. Simply leave blanks next to the verbs you choose not to change.**)

I always thought it was impossible to go sledding without snow. But that was

before I tried "ice blocking." Some friends and I (got) _____ six 10-

pound blocks of ice from a local gas station. Then we (went) _____ to

a nearby park and (took) _____ the heavy blocks to the top of a large

grassy hill. I (saw) _____ my friends as they (moved)

_____ down the steep slope; they (sat) _____ carefully

on towels laid on top of the blocks so they wouldn't (fall) _____ off.

Finally I (got) _____ the courage to try. Down the hill I (moved)

_____ . I hadn't realized that an ice block could (go)

_____ so fast. Then, near the bottom, I (hit) _____ a

bump and (fell) _____ off, rolling over and over in the grass and mud.

Before long, I was (covered) _____ with dirt and grime. I (liked)

_____ "ice blocking," but sledding on snow is definitely much cleaner.

FOLLOW-UP • After you share the results of your work with a classmate, review the section on verbs in your handbook. Pay close attention to the information on *the number of a verb, the tense of a verb, and irregular verbs.*

SUBJECT-VERB AGREEMENT

Writing "Agreeable" Sentences

START-UP • Whenever you use a singular subject and a verb in the present tense (one person, animal, or thing doing something now), the verb must end in an *s* to *agree* with the subject.

> ***Rolfe studies*** his paint job. (*Rolfe* is a singular subject; *studies* is a singular verb in the present tense.)

For a present tense verb to agree with a plural subject (birds, houses, children, geese, etc.), the verb *must not end* in *s*.

> The ***janitors study*** Rolfe's painting mistake. (*Janitors* is a plural subject; *study* is a plural verb in the present tense.)

Underline the subject once and the verb twice in the following sentences. In the space provided, identify the subject and verb as singular (S) or plural (P). Don't be fooled by a prepositional phrase that comes between the subject and the verb. The verb must agree with the subject, not the nearest noun or pronoun. (Refer to "Subject-verb agreement" in your handbook index for more information.)

Example: ____*P*____ The <u>examiners</u> from the traffic department <u>use</u> the park near my house to test new drivers.

> (*Examiners,* not *department,* is the subject. *Department* is the object of the preposition *from.*)

1. ____*S*____ The <u>examiner</u> <u>tests</u> at least 10 new drivers each day.

2. _____ Most new drivers appear very nervous before their tests.

3. _____ The roads in the park are full of curves.

4. _____ An older man, during his test, stops suddenly in the middle of a road.

5. _____ He then steps on the gas just as suddenly.

6. _____ One nervous teenage girl searches frantically through her purse for her car keys.

7. _____ The examiner in the meantime examines her car.

8. _____ Two happy new drivers leave the testing center with their licenses.

9. _____ A middle-aged woman just misses another car in the parking lot.

10. _____ She looks very nervous behind the wheel of her car.

It is the most exciting, unbelievable . . .

▶ **In a paragraph, recall an exciting or important event from one of your favorite books or movies. Use the *present tense* when you write to help make your paragraph exciting and interesting.**

Example Topic Sentence: *The adventurous Tom Sawyer reenters the dangerous cave to find a hidden treasure.* (*Reenters* is a present tense verb.)

_____

_____

_____

_____

_____

_____

_____

_____

_____

_____

_____

_____

_____

_____

_____

FOLLOW-UP • After you review your paragraph, share your work with a classmate. Check each other's work for subject-verb agreement errors.

SPECIAL AGREEMENT PROBLEMS

Can't we agree on anything?

START-UP • It's not uncommon to find sentences in student writing in which the subjects and verbs don't agree (they aren't both singular or plural). For example, someone might incorrectly write *My dog listen*—a singular subject with a plural verb—rather than *My dog listens*—both singular.

This activity focuses on two particular problems with subject/verb agreement: sentences with collective nouns and sentences in which the subject comes after the verb. (Refer to "Subject-verb agreement" in your handbook index for explanations and examples.)

▶ **Underline the subject (a collective noun) for each set of verbs below; then circle the verb that agrees in number with the subject.**

Example: The <u>crowd</u> in the gym (**is**/are) cheering loudly.

1. Measles (**has**/have) kept several of the best players home all week.

2. The team (**is**/are) required to wash and return their jerseys at the end of the season.

3. The pair of boots I want (**is**/are) in the window.

4. Mathematics (**has**/have) been a challenge to me.

5. The committee (**has**/have) voted in favor of a neighborhood party.

▶ **Underline the subject in each sentence below. (It will come after a helping or main verb.) Then circle the verb that agrees in number with the subject.**

Example: (**Has**/Have) your <u>brother</u> seen that movie?

1. There on the distant horizon (is/**are**) the cloudlike mountain formations.

2. Just beyond that last small town (was/**were**) a large field of prairie-dog burrows.

3. (Has/**Have**) any of your relatives ever been to Colorado?

4. (**Wasn't**/Weren't) Bob and Sandy coming over to baby-sit for your little brother?

5. There (**is**/are) a crowd gathering in front of the school.

FOLLOW-UP • Write sentences using the collective nouns *news, economics,* and *mumps* as the subjects.

ADVERBS: A QUICK REVIEW

Sailing . . . Sailing away!

START-UP • Let's say you are describing the following scene from your science class: As part of a unit on aeronautics, one student, perched on his launching pad, is testing his paper airplane design for the rest of the class. How could **adverbs** help you make this action seem real for a reader? You could say something like, "As soon as Bryan *expertly* snapped his wrist, his sleek airplane sailed *smoothly* and *surely* above the heads of his classmates."

In this example, *expertly, smoothly,* and *surely* are all one-word adverbs. These words help the reader see the launching of Bryan's airplane. Without these three adverbs, the image or picture would certainly not be as colorful and clear. (See your handbook for more on this part of speech.)

▶ **In the following sentences, locate and underline all of the one-word adverbs. (The number of adverbs in each sentence is identified.)** *Note:* **Do not include prepositional phrases used as adverbs.**

Example: The pilot announced, "Thunderstorm activity is <u>quickly</u> building to our left." (1)

1. John's mother hardly dared to look. (1)

2. Someone quietly said that she saw sparks suddenly flicker from one of the engines. (2)

3. John, a seven-year-old boy, excitedly looked around. (2)

4. Soon it was time to land in New York. (1)

5. The passengers filed quickly into the terminal and hurriedly scattered everywhere. (3)

6. John and his mother searched the crowd anxiously for his aunt. (1)

7. Suddenly the airport was without any light. (1)

8. Now to move anywhere was very difficult. (3)

9. The two travelers somehow walked cautiously toward the baggage claim area. (2)

10. They overheard an airport official say, "This is extremely unusual. I have never experienced a power outage here before." (4)

COMPARING WITH ADVERBS

I'm positive. That's comparative.

START-UP • Adverbs, like adjectives, have three forms: *positive, comparative,* and *superlative*. And like adjectives, the spelling of comparative and superlative adverbs depends on the number of syllables in the positive form. For example, if the positive form has one syllable, the three forms go like this: *fast, faster, fastest*. If the positive form has two or more syllables, the three forms go like this: *quickly, more quickly, most quickly*. Check your handbook for more examples.

▶ **Use each of the following adverbs in a sentence. Use the adverb in the form indicated in parentheses. The first one is done for you.**

1. firmly (comparative) __My mom gives orders__

   __more firmly than my dad gives them.__

2. slow (superlative) _____

   _____

3. strangely (positive) _____

   _____

4. frequently (comparative) _____

   _____

5. rarely (positive) _____

   _____

6. loudly (superlative) _____

   _____

7. gently (comparative) _____

   _____

FOLLOW-UP • Share your results with a classmate. Note any of your partner's sentences in which the adverbs are incorrectly formed.

IDENTIFYING DOUBLE NEGATIVES

This couldn't hardly be an adverb!

START-UP • Adverbs describe the action of verbs. They also modify adjectives or other adverbs. Because they are so versatile, writers use adverbs frequently . . . and young writers often end up misusing them.

Using **double negatives** is one adverb-related problem many young writers experience. The problem occurs when two negatives are used where only one is needed.

Double Negative: My mom could*n't hardly* believe what our rented cabin looked like.

Corrected: My mom could *hardly* believe what our rented cabin looked like.

Remember: Avoid using double negatives in your school-related writing (and speaking). They are grammatically incorrect according to the rules governing standard English.

▶ **Underline the double negative in each of the following sentences. Then correct each problem, using only one negative word. Write your corrections above each sentence.**

1. There *was scarcely* wasn't scarcely an inch of floor not covered with dirt.

2. My dad and I weren't barely through the door when we choked on dust.

3. It was Mom's idea to rent a cabin, but she doesn't like nothing to do with cleaning.

4. Then again, she won't never give up on one of her ideas either.

5. There wasn't no sign of light in the cabin, so we started washing windows.

6. My dad never has no rival when it comes to cleaning, and pretty soon sunlight streamed into the little cabin.

7. When we could clearly see the dust balls scattering everywhere and the brown streaks of crud on the sofa, we didn't hardly know what to clean next.

8. But by the end of the day, there wasn't scarcely a speck of dirt left in the place.

9. Next year, my dad and I don't want to rent no cabin for a vacation; we're taking a cruise.

ADJECTIVES AT WORK

It could only happen to me!

START-UP • Let's say you were writing about some-body (possibly yourself) whose pen suddenly popped apart during an essay test. How could **adjectives** help you make this action seem real for a reader? You could say something like this:

> **After the *top* half of Jorge's pen rocketed across the room, the *ink* cartridge and *metal* spring followed in its path. He was left with the *useless bottom* half.**

In this example, the italicized words are all descriptive adjectives. These words help a reader see in his or her mind exactly what has happened.

Special Note: Colorful adjectives add life to writing. They help you tell an effective story. However, don't overuse them; otherwise, your writing will sound forced or unnatural.

Oh! That's so nice and neat.

▶ **Turn to the information on choosing effective modifiers in your handbook and learn about adjectives you should avoid in your writing. (Refer to "Adjective, Colorful" in the index.) List two of these words on the blanks provided below. Beneath each of these words list at least five colorful and creative synonyms. (Don't know what a synonym is? Look it up in your handbook.)**

1. _____

2. _____

▶ **Read and enjoy the following description of a brave, determined artist. Circle eight colorful adjectives in addition to the one already circled in this true story.**

The Blind Seer

Our family's longtime friend, Armand Merizon, is more than an artist. He is a rebel, a man of vision, and something of a prophet.

When I was 13, supposedly asleep in my upstairs bedroom, his (oversized) personality would fill our house. He and my parents would debate for hours about politics, religion, art, and the state of the environment. His roar and his chuckle were so deep they seemed to knock the pictures crooked on the walls. In my mind I could picture his green army coat with its bottomless pockets, his full, black beard that made him look like Fidel Castro, and his far-pointing forefinger. The blue gray smoke from his Jamaican cigar would cloud up through the furnace vents, prick my nostrils, fill my lungs, and cling to my pajamas. I could not have known then how much of him I would take into my life.

Today he is nearly 70 and gradually going blind. Fifty years of experimentation with light and design and texture of paint on canvas are being forced to an early end. He has always filled the center of his canvases with a sparkling, brilliant light. That bright center shows the intense moment in which he sees and feels Beauty. And now it is exactly the center of his vision, the bull's-eye, that he cannot see. Yet he has told me he will not stop painting until his nose touches the canvas.

He used to paint landscapes and seascapes in fine detail. He can't see the details anymore. But now he paints with fierce joy—free forms in colors that make rainbows look pale. Now you can feel his anger and hear his laughter in his abstract designs. He has always rejected society. But now, with his beard turned to gray, he loves life more than ever. And he sees it in excellent detail with his inward eye.

FOLLOW-UP • Share the results of your work with a classmate. (Your answers may vary.) Also share stories about memorable people (excluding immediate family members) in your lives.

USING ADJECTIVES TO COMPARE

My cat's bigger than your cat.

START-UP • Special forms of adjectives are used to compare nouns. When you want to compare two nouns, use the **comparative** form of an adjective:

*I am **taller** than my brother.*

When you want to compare more than two nouns, use the **superlative** form:

*I am the **tallest** basketball player on the team.*

The spelling of comparative and superlative forms depends on the number of syllables in the positive or basic form of the adjective. One-syllable and some two-syllable adjectives form comparatives and superlatives using *-er* and *-est* endings:

big, bigger, biggest

Most adjectives with two or more syllables form the comparative and superlative by pairing the words *more* and *most (less, least)* with the positive form:

terrible, more terrible, most terrible

(Refer to "Adjective, Forms" in the handbook index for more information.)

▶ **Fill in the following blanks with the comparative and superlative forms of the adjectives given. If you are unsure about a spelling, use a dictionary.**

Positive	Comparative	Superlative
great		
large		
smart		
caring		
terrific		
radiant		
weird		
lousy		

Now pretend you are a movie reviewer—like Siskel or Ebert only younger—and in a short paragraph, review your favorite movie. Try to use a number of the adjectives (in one form or another) from the list on the previous page. (Use this page for the final draft of your review.)

Movie Review Paragraph

_____

_____

_____

_____

_____

_____

_____

_____

_____

_____

_____

_____

FOLLOW-UP • Exchange paragraphs with a classmate. Enjoy each other's review. Then circle any comparative or superlative forms used.

REVIEWING PRONOUNS

Greasing Your Writing

START-UP • Pronouns grease your writing. That is, they make your writing run smoothly. Imagine what writing would be like without pronouns:

Tony woke up and thought that Tony would vary Tony's routine and drive Tony's car to work instead of taking the bus.

That sentence runs about as smoothly as an old jalopy. Notice the difference a little "pronoun grease" makes:

Tony woke up and thought that (he) would vary (his) routine and drive (his) car to work instead of taking the bus.

► **There are seven kinds of pronouns:** *personal, relative, indefinite, interrogative, demonstrative, intensive,* **and** *reflexive.* **Review what your handbook has to say about these different kinds of pronouns. (Refer to "Pronoun" in the index.) Then fill in the blanks below.**

1. Personal pronouns take the place of _____ in a sentence.

2. An example of a simple personal pronoun would be _____ .

3. An example of a compound personal pronoun would be _____ .

4. A reflexive pronoun is one that _____

_____ of a sentence.

5. An example of a reflexive pronoun would be _____ .

6. An intensive pronoun _____ or _____ the noun or

pronoun it refers to.

7. Three examples of relative pronouns would be _____ ,

_____ , and _____ .

8. Three examples of indefinite pronouns would be _____ ,

_____ , and _____ .

9. An _____ pronoun asks a question.

10. The four demonstrative pronouns listed in your handbook are _____ ,

_____ , _____ , and _____ .

▶ **Here's some pronoun practice for you. First, underline all of the pronouns in the following selection. Next, write the antecedent (the word the pronoun substitutes for) above each pronoun. The first few are done for you. (*Special Note:* Indefinite pronouns such as *everything* or *anybody* do not have specific antecedents.)**

Last week Mitch turned 17. After getting permission from *Mitch's* his parents, Mitch bought *Mitch's* his first car. *Car* It was a lime green, 1971 Volkswagon Super Beetle. When he brought it home, his parents were a bit surprised.

"I thought you were going to buy a big truck," said his father.

"Well, this was cheaper, and I love the color," replied Mitch.

Mitch's father had owned a Beetle when Mitch was a baby, so they decided to fix it up together. They gave it a good tune-up. Then they checked its seat belts to make sure they were working properly.

"What should we do next?" asked Mitch.

"Since everything is fixed on the inside, we should wash the outside," said Dad.

So the Beetle, as dirty as city snow in March, was cleaned and polished to a glowing green. With fuzzy, purple dice hanging from the rearview mirror, and with the roads clean and dry on an August day, Mitch took his car for its first official spin. He went to the store to pick up milk for his mother.

FOLLOW-UP • Read the selection over to yourself, attempting to use only the antecedents, no pronouns. We think you'll see the need for a little "pronoun grease" here . . . and in your own writing.

PRONOUN PROBLEMS

That's indefinitely a challenge!

START-UP • Words like *everybody* and *everything* are indefinite pronouns that seem to talk about more than one person or more than one thing, right? That is, they seem like plural words. But, in point of fact, pronouns ending in *body* (everybody, somebody), *thing* (everything, nothing) and *one* (someone, no one) function grammatically as singular words—as in "Everybody *has* a blank look on **her** (or **his**) face."

Here are three special pronoun situations, including the one described above, that require careful attention. Read through each situation carefully. Better yet, read through each one with a partner. After both of you understand the problem, supply an example sentence.

1. In your writing, use a singular pronoun to replace an indefinite pronoun ending in *one*, *body*, or *thing*.

    *Does anybody in this class remember the name of **her** great-great-grandmother?* (*Her* replaces *anybody*.)

    *Everything in the lab report is in **its** final form.*
    (*Its* replaces *everything*.)

    Now it's your turn: (Create your own example sentence.)

    _____

2. Use a plural pronoun to replace a compound subject connected by *and* (Mike and Carrie, cat and dog).

    *Mike and Carrie had **their** first dancing lesson.*

    *Between **them**, the cat and the dog do a lot of sleeping.*

    Now it's your turn:

    _____

    _____

3. Use a singular pronoun to replace a compound subject connected by *or* or *nor* when the subject nearest the pronoun is singular.

    *Neither the dogs nor the cat wants **his** ears examined.*

    Now it's your turn:

    _____

    _____

    Use a plural pronoun when the subject nearest the pronoun is plural.

    *Neither the cat nor the dogs want **their** ears examined.*

    Now it's your turn:

    _____

    _____

Write on!

Write one more example sentence for each of the pronoun problems discussed in this activity.

FOLLOW-UP • Review the chart of pronouns at the end of the pronoun section in your handbook to make sure you're familiar with all of the words classified as pronouns.

INTENSIVE AND REFLEXIVE PRONOUNS

Mirror, mirror, on the wall . . .

START-UP • A **reflexive pronoun** acts like a mirror. It reflects back upon the subject of a sentence.

Example: The young man looked at *himself* in the mirror.

An **intensive pronoun** emphasizes or intensifies the noun or pronoun it refers to. Writers use the intensive pronoun as a spotlight to focus attention on the antecedent (the word the intensive pronoun refers to).

Example: She *herself* never carries a mirror with her.

▶ **On the six blanks below, identify the six intensive/ reflexive pronouns listed in the handbook. (Refer to "Pronoun, Types" in the index for help.)**

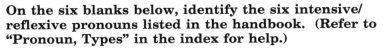

Intensive and Reflexive Pronouns

_____   _____   _____

_____   _____   _____

▶ **On your own paper, finish writing the story started below. It's a story about an attractive little reflexive pronoun named Narcissus. In your story, try to use all six of the pronouns listed above. You may use them as reflexives or intensives. (*Helpful Hint:* See what a dictionary has to say about Narcissus.)**

Once upon a time, there was a reflexive pronoun who loved to look himself

up in his handbook . . .

FOLLOW-UP • Exchange stories with a classmate. Circle each reflexive or intensive pronoun you find. Finally, above each circled pronoun, write whether it is reflexive or intensive.

INTERJECTIONS AND PREPOSITIONS

Oh no! It's another math test.

START-UP • An **interjection** is a word or phrase used to express strong emotion or surprise—*Wow!* or *Yikes!* A comma or an exclamation point is usually used to separate the interjection from the rest of the sentence. A **preposition** introduces a prepositional phrase—a fly *in* his soup. (*In* introduces the prepositional phrase *in his soup*.)

Note: See your handbook for more information on these two parts of speech.

Underline each interjection in the passages that follow. Supply your own interjections in the spaces provided. Also circle any prepositions. (You'll find 10 prepositions in all.)

1. "Good grief, Mr. Decimal, we just had a math test

   on fractions last Friday," complained Ernest.

2. "Hallelujah!" yelled our teacher. "A test a week is good for the soul."

3. "_____ , a test a week is good for indigestion," mumbled Jeff, who

   never got better than a *C* on math tests.

4. "_____ , let's go downtown and get a shake after school," Clarisse whispered

   to me as Mr. Decimal passed out the tests.

5. "SHSHSHSHSHSHSHSHSHSHSH!" voiced Mr. Decimal, looking at us sternly.

6. "Holy fractions, Mr. Decimal. If we were completely quiet every time you gave a test,

   we'd be the quietest eighth graders on earth," I said, smiling sweetly.

7. "Please, Lisa, put a lid on the wisecracks," replied Mr. Decimal patiently.

8. "_____ ! Mr. Decimal isn't that bad," blurted Clarisse while we were

   finishing our shakes, "for a math teacher."

FOLLOW-UP • Team up with a classmate and create a brief scene in which two or more characters express strong emotion or surprise. Consider performing this scene for your classmates.

USING COORDINATE CONJUNCTIONS

Pleasing a Reader's Ear

START-UP • Parallel structures (two or more ideas worded in the same way) are pleasing to our "reading ear." They make us pay special attention to certain words. They add rhythm and music to sentences. They create powerful and important ideas.

Very often, words, phrases, and ideas that are parallel are connected by **coordinating conjunctions** (*and, but, so, for,* and *yet*).

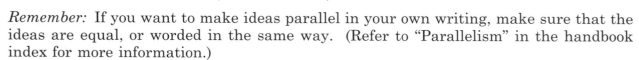

> I hear *and* I forget.
> I see *and* I remember.
> I do *and* I understand.
> (Chinese Proverb)

> The book to read is not the one that thinks for you, *but* the one which makes you think.
> (James McCosh)

Remember: If you want to make ideas parallel in your own writing, make sure that the ideas are equal, or worded in the same way. (Refer to "Parallelism" in the handbook index for more information.)

▶ **Complete the following sentences by adding a word, phrase, or clause that is parallel to the underlined portion of the sentence. (Refer to the sample sentences above for help.)**

1. Summer can be a leisurely time for <u>reading a good book</u> or _____

   _____ .

2. When my friends and I get together for a movie marathon, we usually rent at least

   <u>one horror movie</u>, _____ ,

   and _____ .

3. <u>Packing my suitcase for our vacation</u> is as much fun for me as _____

   _____ .

4. On our family vacation, we always take along three things to make the long drive

   less boring: <u>plenty of paper and pencils</u>, _____

   _____ , and _____ .

5. Labor Day signals <u>the end of summer vacation and</u> _____

_____ .

6. On the first day, we drove all morning and <u>saw nothing but cactus and sagebrush;</u>

then we drove all afternoon and _____

_____ .

SPECIAL CHALLENGE: **Underline the idea that upsets the parallel structure in each of the following sentences. Then rewrite the sentence so that all ideas are parallel.**

Example: A vegetarian is defined as "one whose diet consists of grains, plants, and <u>the products of plants</u>."

A vegetarian is defined as "one whose diet consists of grains, plants, and plant products."

1. Today there are millions of vegetarians in the United States and <u>Europe has</u>

   <u>millions of them, too.</u>

   _____

   _____

2. Pythagorus, a very famous vegetarian, traveled throughout ancient Greece in

   search of truth, knowledge, and <u>what life means</u>.

   _____

   _____

3. Another famous vegetarian, Sir Thomas More, was tried for high treason, found

   guilty, and <u>then they executed him</u>.

   _____

   _____

FOLLOW-UP • Turn to the Preamble to the Constitution in your handbook. (Refer to "Constitution" in the index.) Read it once to yourself and then to a partner. Have your partner do the same. Identify the parallel parts in this famous statement.

FOR YOUR REVIEW • **Subordinate conjunctions** are other important connecting words. They help make *complex sentences*. See a list of these connectors after the "Subordinate Conjunction" explanation in your handbook.

PARTS OF SPEECH REVIEW

Eight is enough.

START-UP • Let's suppose that one day after language arts class, a stranger from a strange land asks you the following questions: What does the term **parts of speech** mean? And why do you have parts of speech? How would you answer this stranger? Think about these questions as you work on this review. Ask a classmate what he or she thinks. Then, as a class, see if you can come up with some good answers.

WARM-UP: *Name one of the eight parts of speech in each of the eight "cuddly faces." Don't look in your handbook (at least, not yet) but, rather, try to name all of them on your own. Then, if the "inkwell" runs dry and you can't think of any more, refer to your handbook.*

► **Pair up with a classmate and, as a team, identify the part of speech for each underlined word. There are five examples of each part of speech, except for the interjection, which has one example. (Refer to your handbook for help.)**

<u>At</u> the beginning of <u>last</u> year, a new girl joined our <u>class</u>. Her name was Kim, but <u>everyone</u> <u>called</u> her "Bigfoot" because of the size of her feet. Some kids <u>occasionally</u> teased her, not just because she was new, <u>but</u> because she was different. She looked as if she <u>were</u> two grades older than we were. Kim is tall and would <u>always</u> look at her feet when she walked. Maybe she was afraid she was going to run them into something.

<u>Since</u> my parents knew her <u>parents</u> from church, they <u>pushed</u> me to be nice to <u>her</u>, to stick up for her and hang around <u>with</u> her. I wasn't thrilled, but Kim turned out to be pretty nice. She helped me with my <u>math homework.</u> She also made some pretty <u>funny</u> <u>remarks</u> <u>about</u> Mr. Wheeler, the gym teacher, <u>when</u> he was out of earshot. One day Kim taped his whistle to his clipboard. It wasn't until <u>he</u> went to reach for it to whistle at Clyde, who <u>was bouncing</u> a basketball <u>repeatedly</u> off Mike, that he noticed what Kim had done. We both laughed so <u>loudly</u> that he knew we were guilty. <u>We</u> got a week's detention <u>for</u> that stunt.

Kim doesn't pull <u>crazy</u> stunts like that anymore. And nobody <u>ever</u> <u>makes</u> fun of her <u>or</u> calls her "Bigfoot" either. She's known as a <u>good</u> <u>friend</u> <u>and</u> all-around nice person. <u>Gee,</u> she should have let <u>us</u> know right <u>from</u> the start.

FOLLOW-UP • Write sentences on your own with examples of the different parts of speech underlined. Then exchange sentences with a classmate and identify the part of speech for each underlined word in your partner's sentences.

READING AND LEARNING STRATEGIES

Getting Your Act Together

Do you find it hard to keep track of important facts and details in reading assignments? Do you dive headfirst into reading material with no plan in mind? Do you sometimes have trouble figuring out the main idea "behind" the reading? Don't worry. If you answer yes to these questions, you're not a "reading wreck." You've just become a little lazy with your reading, or perhaps you've picked up some bad reading habits. Or then again, maybe you never learned how to read factual material. In any case, this section has a number of helpful strategies that will show you how to take charge of your study-reading.

The **Reading and Learning Strategies** cover everything from locating the main idea to finding cause and effect details, from memory techniques to categorizing strategies. There's even an activity that will help you compare apples and oranges. In short, these strategies cover reading from left to right and top to bottom.

Special Note: Refer to "Study-Reading Skills" in your handbook for more guidelines and strategies.

Getting Started

User's Checklist

Check your progress as you work on these **Reading and Learning Strategies.**

☐ **Study-Reading** • *SQ3R*

☐ **Cause and Effect Diagram** • *Pattern Making*

☐ **Problem and Solution** • *Troubleshooting*

☐ **Memory Techniques** • *In 1492, Columbus sailed . . .*

☐ **IMU: Identify, Memorize, Use** • *Rap it up!*

☐ **The Venn Diagram** • *Comparing apples and oranges . . .*

☐ **Using Bar Graphs** • *Picture this!*

☐ **Using Pie Graphs** • *Information in the Round*

STUDY-READING

SQ3R

START-UP • It's one thing to read a sports story in the newspaper . . . and quite another thing to read a chapter in a history or science textbook. One is easy to read; the other is usually more challenging. One is reading for enjoyment; the other is assigned reading for information. How can you best meet the challenges of assigned reading? This activity provides one valuable answer.

The **SQ3R** reading strategy (survey, question, read, recite, review) will help you identify and remember information by reminding you to look carefully before, during, and after the reading. We urge you to use this strategy when the reading material presented to you is really a challenge, loaded with important information.

Begin by reading about SQ3R in *Write Source 2000.* **Then fill in the outline below using the "Managing Stress" page in your handbook. (Refer to "Stress management" in the index.)**

S – Survey

❑ Look at chapter titles, headings, boldfaced words, illustrations, and captions. (List them here if you think it would help.)

❑ If introductions and summaries are brief, read them.

❑ Get a general idea of what this reading material is about.
(Write your own sentence stating this idea.)

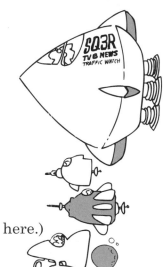

Q – Question

❑ List any questions you may have about this topic.

❑ Turn the chapter title and headings into questions. (Do that here.)

❏ While you read, ask additional questions. (Ask at least two.)
Note: Don't ignore words you don't know. For example, you might ask, "What does 'sibling' mean?"

R – Read

❏ Use an appropriate reading speed and watch for the answers to your questions.

R – Recite

❏ Stop from time to time to recite—in your own words— what you are reading. (Try stopping once and briefly writing about your reading here.)

R – Review

❏ Answer each question you've listed or trade questions with a classmate and answer each other's.

FOLLOW-UP • Share the results of your work with your classmates. Use this reading strategy for the next challenging reading assignment in one of your other classes. See if it helps you to better understand the material.

CAUSE AND EFFECT DIAGRAM

Pattern Making

START-UP • When you read, you must also "look." You must look for patterns among the facts and details to help you better understand the material. There are several common patterns (ways in which the ideas or details are arranged or presented). A number of details may *compare or contrast* one idea with another or provide *solutions to problems*. Still other details may create a *cause and effect* relationship between certain ideas. These are common patterns you must look for when you read.

How do you know what kind of pattern is being created in reading material? Often the titles and subtitles tell you. Sometimes the topic or kind of material lends itself to a particular pattern or patterns. Other times you have to rely on your own good judgment and experience as a reader.

Let's say there seems to be a **cause and effect** relationship between the ideas in your reading. How can you tell for sure? One way is to diagram or write out the points in question. That is what was done with the information on the Civil War below:

Topic: **The Civil War**

Causes (Because of . . .)	Effects (. . . these conditions resulted.)
* Sectional differences - North was largely industrial - South was largely agricultural * Slavery conflict * Developments in politics - Republican Party founded - Lincoln elected * Secession	= 620,000 soldiers died = Bitterness between North & South continues = Beginning of modern warfare - fought under single command - battled from trenches - used repeating arms - used breech-loading arms - used observation balloons - used ships, mines, submarines = End of slavery = Preservation of Union

AFTER • THOUGHT Obviously, a diagram like the model above not only helps you better understand your reading material, but also comes in handy when it's time to review for a test. (See "Word pictures" in your handbook index for other helpful diagrams.)

▶ **Now it's your turn! Read the report on the peregrine falcon in your handbook. (Refer to "Report, Model report" in the index.) Then chart the important *causes and effects* of the peregrine's struggle to survive as an endangered species.**

Helpful Hint: As you read, remember that sometimes the *effects* are discussed at great length and the *causes* merely mentioned; sometimes just the opposite is true. You should also know that sometimes the effects are discussed *before* the causes.

Causes (Because of . . .)	Effects (. . . these conditions resulted.)

FOLLOW-UP • Find an article in a newspaper or magazine that presents facts and details that have a cause and effect relationship. Share the article with your classmates and diagram it as a class.

PROBLEM AND SOLUTION

Troubleshooting

START-UP • Picture this: A mechanic has to find the cause of a mysterious ticking noise in a customer's car engine. This is his problem. How will he solve it? If he is a good mechanic, he'll troubleshoot. That is, he'll go through all of the necessary steps in a very careful way to find the cause of the noise. So . . . what does a car mechanic have to do with you? Read on and find out.

I've got this problem.

If you approach your reading assignments (or just about any assignment) as a troubleshooter, you'll be much more likely to make good use of the material at hand. Let's say you are about to write a play; that is your problem. What you need are some "solutions." That is, you need to better understand how to begin. You turn to "Writing Plays" in your handbook for help. Note how a good troubleshooter organized this reading material to make the best use of it.

Topic: Playwriting

Problem: How can I start writing a play?

Solution:
1. Choose real-life characters based on people you know.
2. Give them a real-life problem to overcome.
3. Put in a message.
4. Use a collection sheet to gather details.

Main Idea: Writing a play doesn't have to be difficult.

 TIP Watch for opportunities to use this strategy in all your classes. The more you practice, the easier it will be to use.

▶ Now it's your turn to troubleshoot. The "problem" is that you have been asked to write a letter to someone you don't know. You must figure out how to solve this problem. Where in your handbook are you likely to find help? Choose the best steps to a "solution." (Refer to "Letters, Fan letter" in the index and read the entire first page of the section you turn to.)

Topic: Writing a Letter to Someone I Don't Know

Problem: How do I write a letter of this kind?

Solution:

Main Idea: I must decide what I need to say, write a clear letter, and send it properly.

FOLLOW-UP • For additional practice, create a "problem" that can be explored using your handbook. ("How do I . . ." or "How can I . . .") Exchange problems with a classmate, find solutions, and discuss the results.

MEMORY TECHNIQUES

In 1492, Columbus sailed . . .

START-UP • Remember that rhyme? Can you finish it? If so, you have a pretty good idea of how memory techniques or strategies work. The key is organizing or personalizing information in such a way that it is easy to remember. By putting historical dates and places into a poem, you will be able to remember them longer.

And there are other strategies you can use. For instance, words that are difficult to spell can be conquered by thinking of them as acronyms. (An *acronym* is a word made up of the first letter [s] of several words in a phrase.)

Create three of your own spelling aids. To do this, simply think of each word as an acronym—an acronym for the sentence you have created. (See the sample below. Also refer to the list of commonly misspelled words in your handbook for possible words to use.)

1. _____ amoeba _____ — <u>A</u>ndy's <u>Mo</u>ther <u>O</u>ften <u>E</u>ats <u>B</u>aked <u>A</u>pples _____

2. _____ rhythm _____ — _____

3. _____ — _____

4. _____ — _____

TIP The mind takes in information and tries to create memorable patterns in which to store it. The more you can do to help your mind create memorable patterns, the more likely it is you will remember information.

▶ Now create a few *acronyms* to help you remember information for a school assignment or test. Record your acronyms and what they stand for on the lines below. (The first one is done for you.) Begin by creating an acronym for remembering the names of the Great Lakes—Superior, Michigan, Huron, Erie, Ontario.

1. _____PREPS_____ – _____This acronym was created to help remember the four freedoms guaranteed by the First Amendment: freedom of the Press, REligion, Petition, and Speech._____

2. _____ – _____

3. _____ – _____

▶ On the lines below, identify an additional *memory aid* you have used to help you remember reading or test material. This might include rhymes, drawings, stories, alphabetical listings, abbreviations, or any other device that works for you. If you haven't used any, make one up now. (Share what works for you with your classmates.)

Personal memory aids:

_____

_____

_____

_____

_____

_____

FOLLOW-UP • Turn to the "Yellow Pages" in your handbook and think of a memory strategy for using a punctuation mark, for identifying a part of speech, or for using one or more plural forms. (Share your ideas with your classmates.)

IMU: IDENTIFY, MEMORIZE, USE

Rap it up!

> Use the IMU strategy to memorize new words, words you must know to understand the reading material. (1) Identify the words you don't know. (2) Memorize the definitions. (3) Use the words.

Step 1: Identify five to ten KEY words from a current reading assignment or chapter in one of your textbooks. (Your teacher may give you this list.)

1.   6.

2.   7.

3.   8.

4.   9.

5.   10.

Step 2: Memorize the definitions. (Use a dictionary or glossary if necessary to write your definitions.) If allowed, you may want to work with a partner: one calls out the word and the other gives the definition.

1.

2.

3.

4.

5.

6.

7.

8.

9.

10.

Step 3: Use the words by writing a rap (or poem) that includes ALL the vocabulary words correctly. Include some definitions if you wish.

 Use the **IMU** strategy for learning key vocabulary words in your reading as well as main ideas, facts, and other important data.

▶ **Write your rap or poem here.**

FOLLOW-UP • You may want to perform your rap (or read your poem) for another classmate, your family, or your class.

THE VENN DIAGRAM

Comparing apples and oranges . . .

START-UP • Being able to see how facts and details compare and contrast with each other is a very useful reading strategy. One way to see or visualize these similarities and differences is to fit them into a Venn diagram. Venn diagrams will help you see and file many important details in a simple, effective way. (See "Venn diagram" in your handbook for an explanation of the basic parts of this reading and learning tool.)

TIP Whenever you compare and contrast two things, you will want to do so in the same category. For example, if you were to compare two presidential candidates, you would want to compare their views on the same topic—the environment, for example. (Comparing views on different topics would be pointless.) Notice below how we've compared and contrasted apples and oranges (both fruit) in various categories: What are they? Can you eat them? Color? Etc.

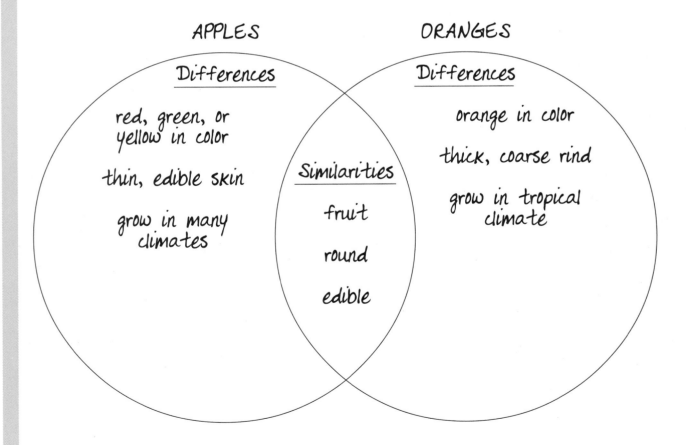

APPLES   ORANGES

Differences   **Differences**

red, green, or yellow in color   orange in color

thin, edible skin   thick, coarse rind

grow in many climates   grow in tropical climate

Similarities

fruit

round

edible

Circling Around

Pair up with a classmate and together read the paragraphs on latitude and longitude in your handbook. (See "Maps" in the index.)

Then give the information in these paragraphs the "Venn" treatment. Here's how to do this:

- Find at least three or four points related only to latitude and write them in the first circle.
- Then find three or four contrasting points that relate only to longitude and place them in the second circle.
- In the space where the circles overlap, identify two or three points or features that are true for both latitude and longitude.

THE VENN TREATMENT

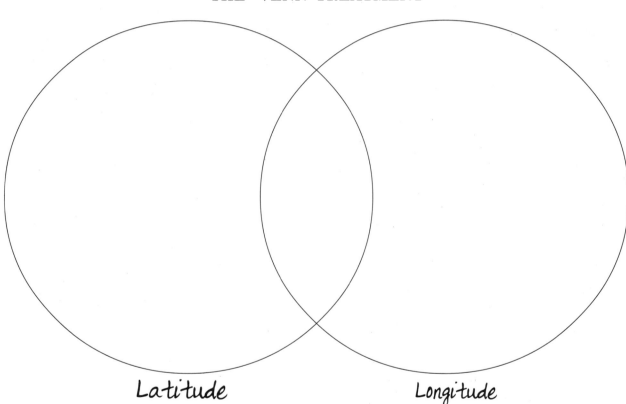

Latitude   Longitude

FOLLOW-UP • Make sure you compare results with your classmates after you finish your diagram. Also, the next time one of your reading assignments seems to be of the comparison-and-contrast type, give it the "Venn" treatment. It will not only help you better understand the reading, but also help you review the material later on.

USING BAR GRAPHS

Picture this!

START-UP • Graphs are used to turn information into a picture so that you can see at a glance what might take several sentences to explain in words. Graphing helps you *analyze* information—that is, it helps you separate the essential facts and show how they relate to one another. If you look in your handbook, you will see that there are three common kinds of graphs. (Refer to "Graphs" in the index.) This activity will help you better understand and use **bar graphs**.

▶ **Carefully study the following bar graph, which shows the number of deaths from heart disease for males between the ages of 55 and 64. Then, on your own paper, answer the questions below. (Discuss your responses with a classmate.)**

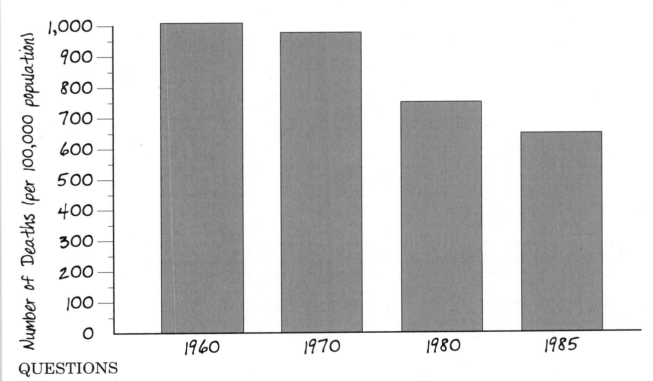

QUESTIONS

1. According to the graph, approximately how many men between the ages of 55 and 64 (per 100,000 of population) died of heart disease in 1960? In 1985?

2. What other pieces of information can you learn from this graph? (List at least two things.) *Remember:* Bar graphs allow you to make comparisons.

FOLLOW-UP • Create a bar graph on your own paper that shows the mean distance between the sun and each of the four Jovian planets. (Refer to "Planets" in the handbook index for this information.)

USING PIE GRAPHS

Information in the Round

START-UP • A **pie graph** shows how each part of something compares to the other parts and to the total "pie." The model pie graph below represents the total area of the earth covered by water, and shows how much of that total is made up by the four oceans. (The numbers are percentages, or the part of the whole expressed in hundredths. For example, the Pacific Ocean is 46/100 of the total area covered by water.)

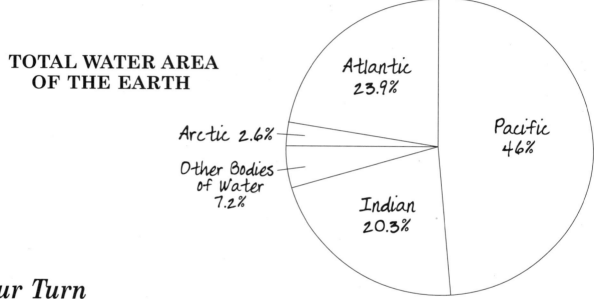

TOTAL WATER AREA OF THE EARTH

Atlantic 23.9%

Arctic 2.6%

Other Bodies of Water 7.2%

Pacific 46%

Indian 20.3%

Your Turn

▶ **Create a pie graph on your own paper that represents the total land area of the earth, and show how much of the land area is made up by each continent. You will find the data for your graph in the map section in the handbook. (Refer specifically to "Topographic Tally Table.")**

Getting Started: To determine how big a piece of the pie you should make for each continent, multiply the percentage of the total land area it covers times 3.6. (There are 360 degrees in a circle.)

For example: Asia is 29.7% of the total land area.

> 29.7 x 3.6 = 106.92 (rounded to 107)

> Asia's portion of the pie graph should take up 107 degrees. Use a compass to mark the appropriate number of degrees in the circle.

Special Note: The percentages for all of the continents actually add up to 99.5%. You can assume that .5% of the total land area is not assigned to one of the continents. Label this tiny slice of the pie graph "other."

TALKING AND LISTENING ACTIVITIES

Learning to Learn

Getting Started

Famous American cowboy humorist Will Rogers once said, "If you're talkin', you ain't learnin'." Rogers' Native American background taught him to respect the words of the speaker, and he himself became one of the best-loved and most famous speakers of his time. Like so many others, Rogers knew that talking and listening were not only important, but inseparable.

Studies show that over 40 percent of what we learn comes from listening to the spoken word. With just under half of what we learn depending on our listening skills, it seems apparent that we need to focus on developing those skills. In the following **Talking and Listening Activities**, you will practice both speaking and listening skills.

It takes practice to be a good writer and reader; it also takes practice to become a good speaker and listener. All four of these skills are essential to effective communication.

Special Note: Refer to the "Speaking and Listening to Learn" section in your handbook for information on preparing speeches, reading out loud, listening, and interviewing.

User's Checklist

Check your progress as you work on these **Talking and Listening Activities**.

☐   **Presenting an Award** • *"No one is more deserving . . ."*

☐   **Introducing a Person** • *"I'm proud to introduce . . ."*

☐   **Oral History** • *"It's been in our family forever."*

☐   **Interviewing** • *"I'm so glad you asked."*

☐   **Focusing on the Topic** • *"I just went to the Bahamas!"*

☐   **Active Listening** • *Action!*

☐   **Listening for Facts** • *Now hear this!*

PRESENTING AN AWARD

"No one is more deserving . . ."

► Think of an award that you would like to give out. This award can be for an actual accomplishment, for something silly, or for some common, everyday thing. Design the award and write an inscription for it. Then write a presentation speech.

FOLLOW-UP • If the award is for someone in your class or family, present it in person. If it is for a person who cannot be reached, ask one of your classmates to accept the award on her or his behalf.

INTRODUCING A PERSON

"I'm proud to introduce . . ."

START-UP • Consider this scenario: In your social studies class, you have worked on family histories and have written about your parents and grandparents. Now your teacher has asked you to give a brief introductory speech about someone in your family.

Choose a parent or grandparent to introduce to the class. Be sure to mention relationship (my mother's father), name, birth date, and occupation. You may also consider the following:

> ❑ What would your parent or grandparent want to tell the class?
> ❑ Which special lifetime event(s) should be highlighted?

Read your introduction for the class (or for your group). Be sure to put some enthusiasm in your voice! (Read over the information in your handbook on writing and delivering a speech before you begin. See "Speech skills" in the index.)

FOLLOW-UP • Explore your thoughts and feelings about the introductory speeches in a free writing. (Write for 5 minutes.) Share the results of your writing with a partner or a group of classmates.

ORAL HISTORY

"It's been in our family forever."

Tell us about a family heirloom or personal treasure (something that is very special to you). Give the history of your treasure and why you think it means so much. You may need to talk to your parents (or grandparents) since they often know the important details about where heirlooms come from, how old they are, why they are considered special, and so on.

FOLLOW-UP • Share at least one other piece of "oral history" that your parents or grandparents shared with you. This will probably be a story about your family, your town, or the way things used to be. Whatever it is, this information will be preserved for future generations only if you keep sharing it, telling the story to friends and new members of your family.

INTERVIEWING

"I'm so glad you asked."

START-UP • One of the most valuable sources of information available to people is other people. And the best way to get information from other people is to sit down, talk to them, and listen carefully. (This is, of course, how reporters get most of their information.)

Interviewing people you do not know can be difficult, but interesting. Interviewing people you do know is easier, but just as interesting. (For instance, I learned in an interview with my own father that just before the atomic bomb was dropped on Hiroshima near the end of World War II, he was aboard a ship in the Philippines, ready to invade Japan!)

▶ **Interview one of your parents or grandparents. Prepare your questions beforehand and leave plenty of room to write. Most people love to talk about their own lives, especially when they know that somebody else cares to listen.**

❏ **If you are the interviewer, you might . . .**

1. Write as many questions as you can about what you think might interest you, your classmates, and the person you are interviewing.
2. Include some questions that ask for personal opinions or reactions.
3. Choose the question you want to start with.
4. Be sure to take notes, but be sure to *look* at the person as much as possible.
5. Review the "Interviewing" section in your handbook.

FOLLOW-UP • Share what you learned in your interview with the rest of the class. State the main points of the interview as well as any information that was new or startling to you.

FOCUSING ON THE TOPIC

"I just went to the Bahamas!"

START-UP • Comedian Steve Martin, in his stage show, often gazes past his audience for a number of seconds without moving, then suddenly shakes his head and remarks, "Oh, sorry, I just went to the Bahamas."

All listeners, from time to time, "go to the Bahamas." While daydreaming has its proper time and place, it is not appropriate during teacher instruction, classroom discussions, review work, or any other time people expect you to listen.

In order to focus your mind, it is important to clear out the "extra" thoughts that interfere with your ability to listen. Work through the exercise that follows to see how to clear your mind and set your focus.

▶ **Answer the following questions as honestly as you can and fill in the blanks. This could be an important first step in becoming an effective listener and a better communicator.**

1. While you were reading the directions for this activity,
    did any other thoughts slip into your mind?   Yes ____   No ____

    a. If yes, what were they? _____

    _____

    b. If no, explain why. _____

    _____

2. What are some topics that do occasionally "creep" into your mind during important listening sessions? List them on the lines provided.

    a. _____   d. _____

    b. _____   e. _____

    c. _____   f. _____

3. Why do you think these topics pop in and out of your mind during the day?

    _____

▶ During a class discussion, consider the *distractions* that can interfere with good listening, the possible *results* of good listening, as well as the positive actions listed in the handbook that help listeners stay in *focus* and *concentrate*. (Refer to "Guidelines, Listening skills" in the index for the list of positive actions.) Then complete the map outline below. (Example responses are given.)

Noises

Avoid daydreaming

Distractions

Ways to Focus

GUIDELINES FOR IMPROVING LISTENING

Results of Good Listening

Gain knowledge

Look at speaker

Concentration Aids

▶ **After listening carefully to the class discussion, list some of your class's ideas of ways to improve listening.**

1. _____

2. _____

3. _____

4. _____

5. _____

FOLLOW-UP • How *was* your listening during this "listening" activity? Was it the same as usual, or do you feel that it was improved? Do you know why your listening may have improved? What can you do in the future to continue improving your listening skills? What specific strategies can you use?

ACTIVE LISTENING

Action!

START-UP · A director will call "Action!" to begin a scene for a movie, and everyone on the set is reminded to focus on the task—acting. As a movie viewer, it is also important to mentally say "action," focusing your attention on the dialogue, a very important part of the movie.

   Listening is an active process. You need to remember that good listening skills don't just happen. They need a concentrated effort to develop properly. Both the listener and the speaker share in the task of communicating—if either one fails, they both fail.

■ When you listen, remember to call **A C T I O N** !

Attention — Clear your mind and get ready to listen.

Concentrate — Listen carefully and focus on what is being said.

Think — Think about what is being said and what it may mean.

Interpret — Decide what the message means—especially what it means to you.

Organize — Organize your thoughts so that the message is as clear and memorable as possible.

Note — Take notes (mentally or physically) on what you've just heard so that you can remember and use it later.

▶ **Now we are going to ask you to act out a brief story with little (if any) time to prepare. Pair up with a classmate and perform an impromptu miniplay (30 seconds or so) for the rest of the class. Simply choose one of the story starters and see what develops. (Obviously, you'll have to listen carefully to what your partner says.) Begin when the teacher calls "Action!"**

Story Starter 1

   Listener 1: *Boy, was it hot today!*

   Listener 2: *How hot was it?*

   Listener 1: *It was so hot* _____

   Listener 2: *No, really? How hot was it?*

Story Starter 2

   Listener 1: *Oh no, we're in plenty of trouble now.*

   Listener 2: *Do you mean the buffalo that are stampeding toward us?*

   Listener 1: *No, even worse. The* _____

Story Starter 3

Listener 1: *I guess it's finally time to go.*

Listener 2: *Already?*

Listener 1: *Yes.*

Listener 2: *Well, this is it. But, _____*

Story Starter 4

Listener 1: *Holy blasting caps, Batman!*

Listener 2: *What is it, Robin?*

Listener 1: *Look at that! Oh no.*

Listener 2: *This could be it for us. _____*

Story Starter 5

Listener 1: *Are you feeling all right?*

Listener 2: *Yes. I guess so.*

Listener 1: *Are you sure? You seem awfully quiet.*

Listener 2: *Well, _____*

Story Starter 6

Listener 1: *The teacher said we had to do what?*

Listener 2: *Get up in front of the room and do a play.*

Listener 1: *But what will we do?*

Listener 2: *How about _____*

FOLLOW-UP • Make note of something you like in each performance. Discuss the results of the performances at the end of the class period. Remember, when the teacher calls "action," the audience must "act" as well—as careful listeners.

LISTENING FOR FACTS

Now hear this!

START-UP • A very important listening skill is the ability to pull important facts out of what you hear and arrange them in a way that will help you understand and remember them.

Write your own fictitious school announcements by filling in the blanks below. Make them informative, but try to keep them interesting and different as well. Keep in mind that announcements go out to large audiences, so be careful not to offend anyone. It is also wise to repeat important information and to use introductory and transition words (people never "hear" the first words of announcements) before key facts.

Note: This could be a great activity to work on with a partner, if your teacher approves. (Be sure to share your announcements with the class, and don't let this form limit you. Make additions and changes as necessary. The blanks may be filled in with any number of words.)

Today's Announcements (Rewrite as needed on your own paper.)

"May I have your attention please for today's announcements.

• A very important meeting of the _____ club will take place in room _____ tomorrow _____ .

• Students who have _____ need to bring _____ on Friday to be ready _____ .

• After the last assembly, it is important to remember _____ .

Please _____ the next assembly.

• The foreign language clubs, both _____ and _____, will meet _____ on _____ . Please bring _____ .

• All teachers, remember _____ on Friday. Also, _____ .

Finally, _____ ."

FOLLOW-UP • Go back and rewrite "Today's Announcements." This time fill in *some* of the blanks with times, places, and names that are bogus (not genuine, real, or possible). ("A very important meeting of the **diner's** club will take place in room **1307** tomorrow **at 3 a.m.**") See how many bogus words you can slip by your listeners.

THINKING WORKSHOPS

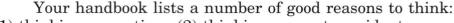

Figuring Things Out for Yourself

Your handbook lists a number of good reasons to think: (1) thinking saves time, (2) thinking prevents accidents, (3) thinking leads to success, (4) thinking can be fun, and so on. But the most important reason is that *thinking helps you figure things out*. And if you're like everybody else, you have lots to figure out.

The **Thinking Workshops** in this section will give you practice *solving problems, making decisions, forming understanding, evaluating information,* and *building arguments—* and they are guaranteed to do so in enjoyable ways. One activity asks you to become a "mentor" for a younger student. Another activity asks you to "walk a mile" in someone else's shoes. Still another asks you to "analyze" your school mascot. You'll find a healthy blend of creative, logical, and clear thinking called for in these workshops, so be prepared to bend your mind in some interesting ways as you work your way through each one.

Special Note: Refer to the "Thinking to Learn" section in your handbook for everything you will need to know about the thinking process. You'll find information about thinking better, thinking and writing, thinking creatively, thinking logically, and using your brain.

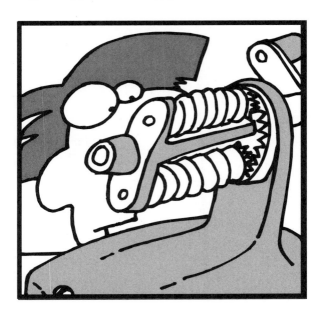

Getting Started

User's Checklist

Check your progress as you work on these **Thinking Workshops**.

■ **Solving Problems**

☐ **Seeing Relationships**
  • *Hidden Connections*

☐ **Summarizing and Applying** • *"What I really need to know . . ."*

☐ **Examining and Predicting**
  • *Time-out!*

■ **Forming Understanding**

☐ **Empathizing** • *Walk a mile in my shoes.*

☐ **Paraphrasing and Inventing**
  • *We the People*

☐ **Thinking Creatively**
  • *What if . . . ?*

☐ **Structures and Analogies**
  • *My Body, U.S.A.*

☐ **Analyzing a Process** • *From Rags to Rigid*

■ **Making Decisions**

☐ **Making Plans** • *"Like a dummy, I said yes!"*

■ **Evaluating**

☐ **Interpreting and Objecting** • *Still waters may be frozen.*

☐ **Comparing, Contrasting, Creating** • *Elephants, Donkeys, and Bears*

☐ **Subjective vs. Objective Judgments**
  • *Chow down!*

■ **Building Arguments**

☐ **Defining Problems, Arguing** • *Fix it or nix it!*

☐ **Summarizing, Judging, Explaining**
  • *Pranks a Lot*

☐ **Mediating and Compromising**
  • *Order on the court!*

SEEING RELATIONSHIPS

FORE • THOUGHT   Here I am, taking an intelligence test. Or is it a test of basic skills? Or an aptitude test? Oh, who cares what it's called. All I know is that they're throwing these lists of words at me and I have to figure out what all the words in the list have in common. Then I've got to choose the one word in the multiple choice section that goes best with the other four. And, finally, they want me to write a sentence that explains the pattern the five words follow. Boy, they don't ask for much, do they?

Hidden Connections

▶ **Take a look at the first problem below. What do the four words have in common? Which word (a, b, c) goes best with the other four? What "pattern" do all five words follow?**

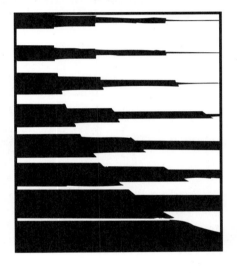

- cloud   a) crutch
- cane   b) unicycle
- bicycle   c) chair
- tripod

   Let's see . . . cloud . . . cane . . . bicycle . . . tripod. Well, bicycle is *two* and tripod is *three* . . . . Oh, I get it. The answer must be *chair*. The pattern is that each word mentions something with one more thing touching the ground than the word before it. Clouds don't touch the ground; a cane touches at one point; a bicycle at two; and a tripod at three. *Chair* must be the right answer because it has four legs, and four comes after three. Hey, this is kind of fun.

   Oh no. The next ones are harder. I think I'm going to need *your* brainpower. Why don't you write in the answers? I'll give you half of my sandwich at lunch! Here, try. Circle the correct answer. (Work in pairs if your teacher allows.)

1. **pea, sea, are, tee**   a) golf
                                    b) eye
                                    c) whale

CONNECTING PATTERN:

Each of the four words has the sound of a letter of the alphabet. So does "eye."

2. **was, bat, tar, star**   a) bad
                                    b) fish
                                    c) ball

CONNECTING PATTERN:

3. **apple, brown, color, dish**   a) slice
b) pie
c) estuary

CONNECTING PATTERN:

_____

_____

_____

▶ **You know what? You're doing so well—why don't you make up one or two of your own and give them to somebody else in the class? Here's some space. Now don't make it too easy!**

4. _____   a) _____

_____   b) _____

_____   c) _____

_____

CONNECTING PATTERN:

_____

_____

5. _____   a) _____

_____   b) _____

_____   c) _____

_____

CONNECTING PATTERN:

_____

_____

AFTER • THOUGHT   Being able to see the relationship between one thing and another is an important part of the problem-solving process. This is especially true when the relationship isn't obvious at first. Look carefully at every part and detail the next time you have to solve a problem.

SUMMARIZING AND APPLYING

FORE • THOUGHT   I hereby assign to you a fifth- or sixth-grade student as a partner—a partner who is about to enter middle school. Your job is to be your partner's "mentor." In other words, your job is to help your partner through those first few weeks at a new school—to talk together about hassles, to help with homework, to encourage your younger partner to figure out what's happening in school.

"What I really need to know . . ."

Now suppose your partner comes to you and says, "You know, what I really need to know is how to think better." Your first reaction is, "That's impossible. I can't teach anyone how to think better." But your partner insists. So you agree to try. "Maybe my handbook can help," you say to yourself. You go to the handbook section called "Thinking Better" and find the list of 10 commands labeled "Becoming a Better Thinker." You read this one-page list *very* slowly and carefully. (After all, you have to *learn* before you can *teach!*)

You decide not to settle for giving general advice. Chances are your partner wouldn't listen if you did. Instead, you think of something *specific* that your partner has to do in school, like

- creating a science project,
- acting in a skit,
- or writing and illustrating a children's book.

Now all that's left for you to do is to get together with your partner and give the practical thinking advice that will improve his or her performance in whichever specific task you've chosen to focus on.

(*Helpful Hint:* As you read the advice in your handbook, take good notes on what you will say during that 15-minute session with your partner.)

AFTER • THOUGHT   Now practice your "teaching session" with a classmate. (*Hint:* You may want to put special emphasis on one of the 10 points, one that seems more important than all the others. Also, based on your experience as a thinker, what would you add if you were asked to write command #11?)

EXAMINING AND PREDICTING

THE SHORT TERM: Suppose all clocks suddenly stopped working. What kind of problems or confusion would this cause?

► **List below as many activities as you can that would be immediately affected during the course of a typical day. For example, your teachers wouldn't know when it was time for lunch, and you wouldn't know if Pizza Hut really served five-minute pizzas. (Have another piece of paper ready just in case you need more room.)**

Time-out!

THE LONG TERM: Suppose clocks never started working again.

► **List five (or more) ways in which our lives would be different.**

1.

2.

3.

4.

5.

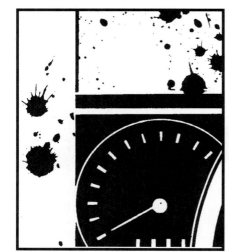

AFTER • THOUGHT   Write a story or description of school, a sport, or home life in a world with no clocks.

EMPATHIZING

FORE • THOUGHT   According to a true old saying, you can't understand me until you have "walked a mile in my shoes." "Walking a mile in my shoes" really means having "empathy," or feeling my feelings as if they were your own. Developing empathy is an important step in coming to understand and respect another person, especially someone who is much different from you.

Walk a mile in my shoes.

Think of what it would be like to be homeless, to not have a bed or room or home to go to at the end of the day, to always have to worry about the weather, food, your safety. How well do you think you would cope?

Put yourself in the shoes of a homeless person and walk for a mile or two. And, as you do, keep a journal. Record what you see, where you go, whom you talk to, how you feel, what problems you run into.

HANDBOOK HELPER

You can find special advice on keeping a journal in *Write Source 2000.* See "Journal writing" in the index.

AFTER • THOUGHT   Find a newspaper or magazine article about the homeless and bring it to class to share with the others. Or talk to someone who works with the homeless or was once homeless. Try to truly "empathize."

PARAPHRASING AND INVENTING

FORE • THOUGHT   By 1791, two years after the United States Constitution went into effect, the first U.S. Congress had passed 10 amendments (formal additions) to the Constitution. These 10, taken together, are known as the Bill of Rights and guarantee that every citizen of the United States has certain basic liberties: the right to practice one's own religion, the right to speak freely, the right to gather in peaceful groups, and so on.

We the People

You will find the "Bill of Rights" listed in the index of *Write Source 2000*. Choose the amendment that interests you the most. Read the amendment carefully and discuss with another person what you think it means.

▶ **After you thoroughly understand it, "translate" the amendment into modern language that speaks clearly to you.**

Translation:

AFTER • THOUGHT   What if Congress and the president decided to drop the Bill of Rights from the Constitution? Imagine what would happen with no freedom of religion, no freedom of the press, no freedom to assemble, no freedom of speech, etc. Use your imagination.   From a student's point of view, write a detailed description of what your world might be like five years after all the guarantees in the Bill of Rights were removed.

THINKING CREATIVELY

FORE • THOUGHT   Do you ever have trouble coming up with "creative" ideas? Well, the *Write Source 2000* handbook (and the activity below) can help. Turn to the "Thinking Creatively" section in your handbook and read the first two pages.

What if . . . ?

▶ **After reading the "What if . . . ?" section, create a new example to go with each of the "What if . . ." questions. (The first one is done for you.)**

1. What if . . . *the telephone had not yet been invented? What if it had been invented just last week?*

2. What if . . . _____

   _____

   _____

3. What if . . . _____

   _____

   _____

4. What if . . . _____

   _____

   _____

5. What if . . . _____

   _____

   _____

6. What if . . . _____

   _____

   _____

7. What if . . . _____

_____

_____

8. What if . . . _____

_____

_____

9. What if . . . _____

_____

_____

10. What if . . . _____

_____

_____

AFTER • THOUGHT   Add two or three "What if's" of your own. Remember, to think creatively, "sometimes you gotta break the rules."

STRUCTURES AND ANALOGIES

FORE • THOUGHT A city is one of the most complicated things in the world. But suppose you had to describe it to a class of kindergartners. How would you explain the communication systems, the transportation systems, the government system, and so on? You couldn't use big words. You would have to make difficult ideas easy to understand.

My Body, U.S.A.

Suddenly you have a bright idea: you will compare a city to a human body! Each of the city's main systems is similar to something in a body. See if you can think of something in the body that corresponds to each of these parts of a city:

streets and alleys
electrical wiring
water towers and pipes
cars and trucks
houses and offices

the mayor
a school
parks and playgrounds
satellite dishes, antennas
grass, trees, and flowers

▶ **In the space below, write the speech you will give to the kindergartners. In your speech, use analogies with the human body to explain what a city is. (Continue on your own paper.)**

A city is like a human body _____

_____

_____

_____

_____

_____

_____

_____

AFTER • THOUGHT Try making an analogy between a city and something other than a body. For example, how is a city like a marching band? How is it like a car? How is it like an essay? How is it like an apple? How is it like a tree?

ANALYZING A PROCESS

FORE • THOUGHT   The words you are reading at this very moment are, obviously, printed on paper. This paper may have started out as old newspapers or old rags. The rags were turned into paper. And when the paper is used up, it may be turned into, say, a rigid cardboard box. A real "rags to rigid" story, you might say!

From Rags to Rigid

Many, many people are involved in the recycling process: collectors, buyers, sellers, truck drivers, etc. Do you have any idea how many people are involved?

Let's have a contest. Try to picture a three-stage recycling process, from rags to paper to cardboard. You decide whether you want to compete against yourself ("Solitaire") or against one other person ("One-on-One"), or whether you'd rather have a team of two or more contestants against another team ("Rumble").

The rules for this contest are simple:
1. **List as many people as you can possibly think of that are in *any* way involved in the making, transportation, sale, or use of recycled paper, anywhere in the process from "rags to rigid."**
2. **STOP after 15 minutes.**
3. **The team with the longest (correct) list WINS!**

AFTER • THOUGHT   You could create special rules to make your contest more interesting. For example, you could set a time limit of 2 minutes and use a stopwatch. Do it again for "Round 2" and "Round 3." How about challenging another class or a different grade? How about creating a special trophy out of recycled materials and awarding it to the winners? How about having a similar contest with recycled plastic?

MAKING PLANS

"Like a dummy, I said yes!"

▶ Read and react to "Balloon Shaving" with a partner. (One of you might read it out loud while the other person listens carefully.) Afterward, list the things Janet and Lea did to plan for the booth. Share your results with the rest of your class and come to some agreement on what they did right or wrong in their planning.

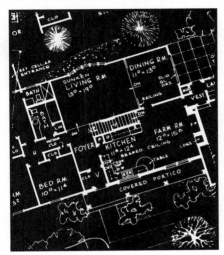

BALLOON SHAVING

The Winter Carnival committee asked Janet to set up the balloon-shaving booth, and, "like a dummy," she said yes. Now it's two weeks before the carnival. "Eek," she says to her friend Lea's mother, "what am I going to do?"

Lea's mother asks her questions like "What is your deadline? How much responsibility did the committee give you? How did they run the booth last year?" That gets her started. But Lea, who is a good friend, helps her see the bigger picture *and* the smaller details.

"What are you after in the long run?" she asks. "Let's try to top last year's booth. And let's go for the best-booth prize. And let's try to make more than $80 for our class banquet." By setting goals, they pump up their enthusiasm. Then they lie around dreaming how the booth will be decorated and how Janet will run it.

To make it just the way they envision it, they break down the project into major parts: (1) getting materials, (2) lining up people to help in the booth, (3) decorating the booth, (4) setting up rules for shaving balloons and winning prizes, (5) cleaning up. Once they have that sorted out, they list the details under each heading. One good thing about Janet and Lea is that they keep checking themselves—"Are we forgetting anything? Do you think that'll work?" They never lose sight of their overall goals.

When the carnival gets close, they try to visualize anything that might go wrong. "What if the shaving cream splatters onto the face-painting booth next door?" (Build higher walls.) "What if it splatters into a little kid's eyes?" (Let's make them all wear plastic swimmer's goggles.) They think of everything. Needless to say, when the carnival arrives, they are ready—and they have a "blast."

AFTER • THOUGHT Ask someone—your mother, teacher, coach, neighbor—how he or she makes plans for an important event. Report your findings to the class.

INTERPRETING AND OBJECTING

FORE • THOUGHT   I remember young Ms. Sisboom, my fourth-grade teacher, who always said, "Smile! It increases your face value." And then there was old Mr. Niblick, the crossing guard, who always wore golf pants and liked to say, "Look before you leap," as if that were the answer to everything.

Still waters may be frozen.

Think back. Did you ever have a teacher (uncle, friend, neighbor) who had a favorite saying? How about "It takes all kinds," or "Might doesn't make right"?

- Write down the favorite saying here:

_____

_____

- Now try to remember a specific time when this person used that phrase. In this space, try to **interpret** and **explain** exactly what he or she meant by using the saying in that situation:

_____

_____

- Now for the fun part. Think of an *exception,* a situation in which the saying would *not* hold true. For example, if a child were trapped under an automobile and an incredibly strong man stepped out of the crowd and lifted it off the child, we could say that in that case "might makes right." Be creative! Explain your exception (or objection) to the favorite saying in this space:

_____

_____

- Invent a new saying that includes the exception you've pointed out. For example, you could say, "Might may not make right, but it makes some things a whole lot easier." Write your new saying here:

_____

AFTER • THOUGHT   Write a short, tactful (not insulting) letter to that former teacher (uncle, neighbor, friend) explaining the exception you've found to his or her favorite saying. End your note by challenging the person to adopt your new saying. (In *Write Source 2000,* you'll find helpful comments on writing a "friendly letter.")

COMPARING, CONTRASTING, CREATING

FORE • THOUGHT In case you haven't noticed, the elephant is the symbol for the Republican Party; the donkey is the symbol for the Democratic Party. It's easy to see the difference between an elephant and a donkey, but do you know the difference between a Republican and a Democrat?

Elephants, Donkeys, and Bears

Find out the differences between Republicans and Democrats by investigating for yourself. Find one person of voting age who claims to be a Republican and another who claims to be a Democrat. Ask each one what he or she thinks is the main difference between the two parties.

Thinking It Through

■ Here are some questions you might ask when you interview your two voters:

❑ Which party tends to favor wealthier people and which tends to champion the middle class and poor?

❑ Which party tends to favor businesses and which looks out more for consumers?

❑ Which party is more likely to suggest new social programs?

❑ Which party favors a more active government and which wants government to get off people's backs?

TIP Using these questions as a guide, it might be a good idea for you to create your own questionnaire and ask a larger number of voters to fill it out.

■ Once you've collected your responses, and as you prepare to write your conclusions, ask yourself these questions:

❑ Did the Republican and Democrat voters agree with each other about anything?

❑ Do you think they gave you an accurate picture of the differences between the two main political parties?

❑ What questions would you still like to clear up?

After you have finished your interview or questionnaire survey, use the space below to report on the answers you received. Then, in a conclusion, write what *you* think is the difference between the two parties. You will probably be left with some questions. Don't be afraid to ask them in your conclusion.

Republicans:

Democrats:

Conclusion:

AFTER • THOUGHT **Invent** a new political party. **Name** it; **choose** an animal to be the symbol for your party; and, on your own paper, **write** a speech to deliver to the delegates at your party's national convention. In your speech, explain how your party will be different from either the Republicans or the Democrats.

SUBJECTIVE VS. OBJECTIVE JUDGMENTS

FORE • THOUGHT   One day Lona Ramirez, Mei-Ling Chen, and six friends were arguing about the lunches in their school's cafeteria. Everybody had a different opinion. After their advisor, Ms. Sturdevant, heard them arguing, she helped them form a committee to evaluate the school's lunches.

"Be careful," she told the committee. "Some judgments we make are purely personal. We call those **subjective** judgments. When you say a grilled cheese sandwich is 'lousy,' for example, your subjective judgment shows your feelings but not much else. An **objective** judgment, on the other hand, focuses on the object itself. It says something specific and can be tested. For example, we might say that a grilled cheese sandwich is made with a stale-tasting, artificial cheese product instead of real cheese. We can test whether that's true or not. We can't test whether something is 'lousy.' "

"Subjective judgments are weak," Ms. Sturdevant said, "so let's keep our judgments as objective as possible."

Chow down!

Then Ms. Sturdevant gave her committee the following list of judgment words and told her students to sort out the objective words from the subjective ones:

well seasoned	*yucky*	*great*
high in calories	*yummy*	*disgusting*
high cholesterol	*sugar-free*	*delicious*
scrumptious	*attractive*	*slimy*
awesome	*boring*	*okay*
low cholesterol	*undercooked*	*warm*
horrible	*nutritional*	*balanced*
stale	*lukewarm*	*bland*
properly cooked	*gross*	*fresh*

Your Turn

Think about the lunches served at your school. (If you don't have a cafeteria, evaluate whatever kind of lunch you bring to school.) Go through Ms. Sturdevant's list above. Pick out and list below only the *objective terms* that match your lunches. Do *not* list subjective terms or objective terms that don't match your lunches. (You need not use all the spaces.)

1)_____   4)_____

2)_____   5)_____

3)_____   6)_____

AFTER • THOUGHT   Compare your list to somebody else's and discuss any differences you discover.

DEFINING PROBLEMS, ARGUING

FORE • THOUGHT   As you walk or ride your bicycle around your town or neighborhood, do you ever spot things that seem to be falling apart? A rusty water tower, a crumbling bridge, a graffiti-covered wall, a cracked sidewalk, a sign blasted by a shotgun, . . . ?
   What should be done?

Fix it or nix it!

Here are four options: (1) **leave** it as it is, (2) **repair** it, (3) **replace** it, or (4) **destroy** it. Make up your mind about which option you would support.

Write a letter to the editor of the local newspaper arguing for your solution to the problem. In your letter, describe the problem, tell why it's important to you and to others, suggest in detail what should be done, and tell what you think the benefits would be. (*Note:* For a model letter to the editor, see "Letter to an Editor" in *Write Source 2000.* Look in the editorial pages of a real newspaper for other models.)

 Before starting your letter, you may want to list your ideas. Here are some basic questions. (Remember the 5 W's and H?)

What (when/where) is the problem? _____

_____

Why is it worth solving? _____

_____

How can it be solved? _____

_____

What would the benefits be? _____

_____

AFTER • THOUGHT   After you have written your letter, pair up with a classmate and exchange your work. Then write another letter to the editor suggesting—in polite terms—that your partner's ideas are nuts!

SUMMARIZING, JUDGING, EXPLAINING

FORE • THOUGHT   We all know what a prank is. We also know that some pranks are good and some are bad. A good prank makes everybody laugh, even the victim. A bad prank—like blowing up a toilet bowl with a big firecracker—hurts people or property and makes everyone feel worse afterward.

Pranks a Lot

Have you ever pulled a prank or had one pulled on you? Have you witnessed or heard about a prank at your school? Describe the prank here, step-by-step, including the general situation, the preparation, the action, and the result.

The Situation:

The Preparation:

The Action:

The Result:

Exchange your work with a classmate and read each other's "prank paper." (Ask for more information about the prank if necessary.) Now, suppose your school decides to put the prankster on trial. You are appointed to be the judge in the case of "the student prankster." Imagine that you have just heard the prosecuting attorney (the one who has to prove the prankster's guilt) make a final statement, followed by the defense attorney's statement (trying to prove the prankster's innocence). Now you must reach a decision: Is the prankster innocent, making this a good prank, or guilty, making this a bad prank? (Refer to the introduction on the previous page for the definition of good and bad pranks.)

■ First, summarize the two opposing arguments you heard.
■ Second, state your verdict.
■ Third, explain your reasoning.

Summary of Prosecution ("Bad Prank") Argument:

Summary of Defense ("Good Prank") Argument:

Your Verdict:

Your Argument in Support of Your Verdict:

AFTER • THOUGHT   Usually an argument will be stronger if you *concede* points to the opposition. (This means you admit that an opponent's point is strong, but you feel yours is stronger.) Can you think of any concessions you should make as you are summarizing the reasoning behind your verdict?

MEDIATING AND COMPROMISING

FORE • THOUGHT   Suppose your school has always gotten big crowds out to see the boys' basketball team play and smaller crowds to watch the girls' team.   Therefore, the school has always charged $3.00 for tickets to the boys' games and only $1.50 for tickets to the girls'.

NOW SUPPOSE THAT YOU ARE THE SCHOOL PRINCIPAL.   You receive two letters from angry parents.   The first letter says it is unfair and "sexist" that the girls' ticket price is lower than the boys'.   The second letter says that the policy had better not be changed, because the girls' team needs all the support from the school that it can get.   It is up to you, the principal, to "mediate" their dispute.   In other words, you have to stand between the two parties in the argument and hammer out some sort of solution.

Order on the court!

Can you think up a compromise plan that will make both sides feel that they have been treated fairly?

■ To help yourself think through the issues, jot down your thoughts on your notepad.   Use the following starters to get your ideas flowing.

NOTES:

The main thing I want for both teams is . . .

Here are the things I can't change . . .

The most important principle in my decision is . . .

Here's the best solution I can think of . . .

Thinking It Through

■ Here are some questions to consider before you finalize your plan:
  - Does your plan treat both sides equally?
  - Will both sides be happy with your compromise?
  - Is your plan the best compromise that could be made?
  - Does your plan correct the unfairness of the past?
  - Will your plan work?

AFTER • THOUGHT   Get together with a classmate and compare notes.   Combine your best ideas and share them with the class.   (Afterward, discuss what you have learned about "mediating and compromising.")

VOCABULARY AND WORD PLAY ACTIVITIES

Language Building

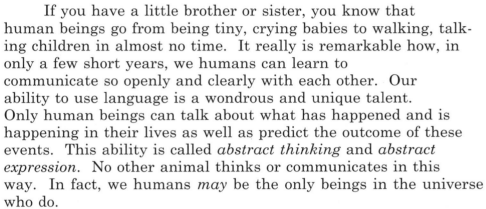

If you have a little brother or sister, you know that human beings go from being tiny, crying babies to walking, talking children in almost no time. It really is remarkable how, in only a few short years, we humans can learn to communicate so openly and clearly with each other. Our ability to use language is a wondrous and unique talent. Only human beings can talk about what has happened and is happening in their lives as well as predict the outcome of these events. This ability is called *abstract thinking* and *abstract expression*. No other animal thinks or communicates in this way. In fact, we humans *may* be the only beings in the universe who do.

In the following **Vocabulary and Word Play Activities**, you will "play" with words. This doesn't mean that words are mere toys, but rather that language is so special it should be celebrated and enjoyed. When you play with your language, you are participating in a very privileged amusement. And when you build your word and language skills, you are improving your already exceptional talents of speaking and writing.

User's Checklist

Check your progress as you work on these **Vocabulary and Word Play Activities**.

☐ **Appreciating Words** • *A Way with Words*

☐ **Poetry** • *Playing with Poetry*

☐ **The Sound of Words** • *Alliteration Alert*

☐ **Bombastic Proverbs** • *"Don't put off till tomorrow . . ."*

☐ **Finding Categories** • *Noun* • *Sense*

☐ **Using Word Parts** • *A Part•ial Solution*

☐ **Using Prefixes** • *Look before you leap.*

☐ **Using Roots** • *It's Greek (and Latin) to me!*

☐ **Vocabulary** • *Concentration*

☐ **Using Flash Cards** • *"I remember a quick flash!"*

APPRECIATING WORDS

START-UP • The best way to improve your vocabulary is to read, and read often. And to increase your vocabulary even further, you should look for "new" or interesting words that pop up along the way.

A Way with Words

▶ Select an article in a newspaper or magazine and read it with a critical eye. Pay particular attention to the kinds of words the writer is using and be on the lookout for any sentence, phrase, or word you feel is especially effective. Write them on the lines below. Also, look for any "new" words that you did not know before you read the article. Share those words with your classmates and add them to your "personal vocabulary list."

Effective sentences, phrases, words:

_____

_____

_____

_____

_____

New words:

_____

_____

_____

_____

_____

_____

FOLLOW-UP • Keep a place in your notebook or journal for new words you come across in your reading. Learning words this way (in context) is one of the best ways to build your personal vocabulary.

POETRY

START-UP • Poetry is a sophisticated kind of word play. However, poetry doesn't always have to be "deep" or of lasting importance. Poetry can be just a great way for young writers to get their hands on words, to hear the sounds and rhythms, to play with the meanings. For example, take a look at the following poem:

> Betsy
> Blonde, Bearded
> Bounces, Bandies, Barks
> Testy, Twittering
> Terrier

The pattern of this poem is as follows:

1st line:	Subject (noun)
2nd line:	Two words describing subject (adjectives)
3rd line:	Three words describing action of the subject (verbs)
4th line:	Two words describing subject (adjectives)
5th line:	One word that brings the thought to a close

Playing with Poetry

Now you try it. Don't worry about coming up with something MEANINGFUL in a world-shaking way, but do try to be creative.

1st line: _____

2nd line: _____

3rd line: _____

4th line: _____

5th line: _____

SPECIAL CHALLENGE: This time you will share the same "subject" with the rest of the class. (Put your poem on your own paper.)

1st line: *War*

FOLLOW-UP • Be sure to share your poems with one or all of your classmates (depending on your teacher's wishes). Appreciating words and poetry is really a group activity.

THE SOUND OF WORDS

START-UP • Alliteration is *the repetition of a sound at the beginning of two or more neighboring words.* Example: Are aardvarks allergic to alliteration? *Note:* Usually alliteration is made up of consonant sounds, but not always.

Question: Are aardvarks allergic to alliteration?

❏ Yes ❏ No ❏ Maybe so

Obviously, we will never know if aardvarks are allergic to alliteration; but after the following activity, you will know whether *you* are allergic to alliteration or actually enjoy using it.

Alliteration Alert

▶ **Note the alphabet letters below. For each one, think of a sentence in which almost all of the words begin with the specified letter. Write your sentences on the lines provided.**

A *Are aardvarks allergic to alliteration?*

B _____

_____

C _____

_____

D _____

_____

E _____

_____

F _____

_____

G _____

_____

H _____

_____

FOLLOW-UP • Continue with other alphabet letters. Experiment! Start each sentence with "I like . . ." or "Never . . ." or "Why. . . ."

BOMBASTIC PROVERBS

START-UP • "Don't put off till tomorrow what you can do today." Or, as Will Rogers once said, "Don't put off till tomorrow what you can do the day after tomorrow." Either way, these sayings or proverbs carry with them "advice about life." A **bombastic proverb** is a proverb that has been *blown up* with so many big words that it's difficult to figure out what advice is being given.

"Don't put off till tomorrow . . ."

How many of the following bombastic proverbs can you match to the original proverb?

_d_ 1. Do not traverse a structure erected to provide passage over a waterway prior to your arriving there.

2. A hard mass that progresses by turning over and over upon its surface without slipping does not successfully gather together a delicate, cryptogamous plant.

3. A canine that gives vent to his sentiments by a series of vocal efforts rarely finds use for his bicuspids.

4. Accelerated execution often produces faulty results.

5. One feathered biped imprisoned in the digits is equal at least to twice that many at large.

a. A bird in the hand is worth two in the bush.

b. Haste makes waste.

c. A rolling stone gathers no moss.

d. Don't cross the bridge before you come to it.

e. His bark is worse than his bite.

Now you're on your own. See if you can figure out the original proverb for each bombastic proverb given below:

1. It is not advantageous to place the sum total of your chicken coop collections in the same wicker receptacle.

_____

2. Never calculate the possible number of your juvenile poultry until the usual period of incubation has been fully accomplished.

_____

3. The warm-blooded, feathered, egg-laying, vertebrate animal that is among the first to awaken (or arrive) invariably comes into possession of the small, legless, invertebrate crawling animal.

_____

FOLLOW-UP • Write your own "bombastic proverb" using the following proverb: "Look before you leap."

FINDING CATEGORIES

START-UP • Wake up your brain! At least awaken the part where you have nouns stored! Look around the room, glance at a magazine, go for a walk—do whatever you have to do to get those nouns flowing strong and steady.

Noun • Sense

STEP 1: List as many nouns (persons, places, things) as you can under "My Nouns" below.

STEP 2: Think of a category (a group) into which each noun would fit. Write the category in the third column.

STEP 3: Fold your paper along the dotted line so your list of categories can't be seen. Ask a classmate to fill in the "Partner's Categories" column, naming a category for each noun.

STEP 4: Compare your lists. Do some words fit in more than one category? Could some categories be stated differently?

My Nouns	My Partner's Categories	My Categories
veal		meat
A Day No Pigs Would Die		book
merry-go-round		ride

FOLLOW-UP • Challenge yourself! Search your mind for some real "finds," some unexpected and distinctive nouns that come to you after some thoughtful searching. Create another list with these words. Also think of a category into which each noun would fit.

USING WORD PARTS

START-UP • Many words in our language are made up of word parts: prefixes, suffixes, roots. Just as you can figure out the meaning of a word when you know the meaning of its parts, you can also guess the meaning of the parts when you know the meaning of the word.

A Part•ial Solution

▶ **Fill in the spaces below with as many words and definitions as you can. If possible, think of words that incorporate each part, without the help of your handbook. Guess at the meanings of the word parts by thinking about familiar words that include the parts. Finally, look up the parts in your handbook to see how accurate your guesses were and to help you complete the chart. A dictionary will be helpful, too. (See "Vocabulary, Improving" in the handbook index.)**

Word Part	*Sample Words*	*Definitions*
circum- (around)	circumnavigate	to go completely around
	circumscribe	
-nomen- or **-nomin-** (name)		
retro- (back- wards)		
-ize (make)		
intra- (within)		

FOLLOW-UP • Anytime you come across a word you don't know, look for word parts you recognize.

USING PREFIXES

START-UP • Thousands of the most commonly used words in English begin with prefixes. One of the greatest things about prefixes (and suffixes and roots) is being able to guess the meaning of a word by knowing the meaning of the prefix. After you learn the meanings of the most common prefixes, you'll be like an archaeologist studying your own language. Just as Indiana Jones can decipher hieroglyphics (language markings) on a cave wall, you will be able to discover the meaning of an unfamiliar word by examining the meaning of its parts. So pull your hat down over your left eye, unstrap your whip from your hip, and take a crack at the following prefix activity.

Look before you leap.

Refer to the "Prefixes" section of your handbook and write the meanings of the following prefixes. Then think of a word that begins with that prefix. DO NOT use the words given as examples in your handbook. Instead, use a dictionary.

Prefix	Meaning	Sample Word
a/an	not, without	apathy
acro		
ante		
cata		
dys		
epi		
hyper		
hypo		
infra		
macro		
mal		
neo		
pseudo		

▶ **Using what you have just learned, match the following words with the proper definitions of each. Circle the prefix in the words to make it easier.**

Group 1

_____ 1. a word formed from the first letters of words in a phrase

a. dyslexia

_____ 2. an underground chamber or tunnel

b. acronym

_____ 3. an exaggeration used as a figure of speech

c. catacomb

_____ 4. a disease, a disorder, or an ailment

d. pseudonym

_____ 5. an imaginary name used by an author, a pen name

e. malady

_____ 6. underlying base or foundation

f. infrastructure

_____ 7. to precede in time

g. hyperbole

_____ 8. impairment of the ability to read

h. antedate

_____ 9. a person with elevated taste in food and wine

i. epicure

Group 2

_____ 1. one skilled in feats of balance, especially at great heights

a. neophyte

_____ 2. a large waterfall or a great downpour

b. hypogeal

_____ 3. the outer layer of skin

c. macrocosm

_____ 4. an imaginary place of misery

d. acrobat

_____ 5. of the period before the Civil War

e. cataract

_____ 6. a recent convert or beginner

f. dystopia

_____ 7. the entire world, universe

g. epidermis

_____ 8. living under the ground

h. antebellum

FOLLOW-UP • Find one new word for at least eight of the prefixes and make up your own matching exercise. Exchange your homemade exercise with a classmate.

USING ROOTS

START-UP • Have you ever heard of a family tree . . . you know, that massive list of all the people you're related to arranged in just the right way to show how you're all related? Well, you might not know that languages are also related to one another. For instance, English, French, and Italian are all descendants of Latin. In turn, many Latin words are descended from Greek words. That means that many English words can be traced back to Latin and Greek roots. Getting to know some of these roots and their meanings will help build your vocabulary and will generally give you a better understanding of your language.

It's Greek (and Latin) to me!

▶ **Define the roots on the lines below; refer to the "Roots" section of your handbook for help.**

phobia _____   viv _____

soph _____   ignis _____

liver, liber _____   am _____

morph _____   phil _____

nounce _____   neur _____

simil _____   trib _____

▶ **Look up the following words that have grown from the roots you just learned. Note how the meanings of the roots contribute to the meanings of the words.**

philosophy _____

_____

revive _____

_____

amicable _____

_____

denounce _____

_____

vivacious _____

_____

Now, how many other words can you think of that have one (or both) of the roots present in "philosophy"?

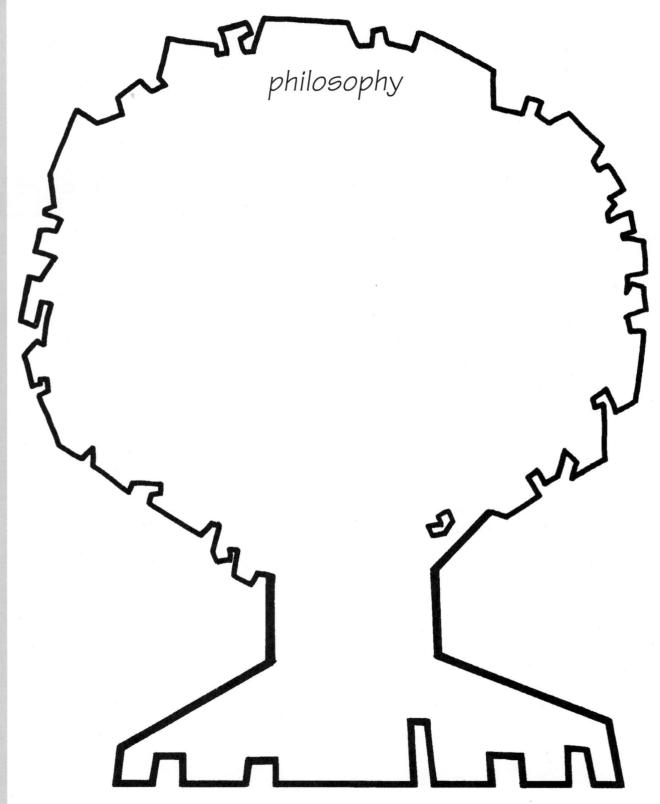

philosophy

FOLLOW-UP • Work up family trees for other words you come across in your studies.

VOCABULARY

Concentration

(1) Get together with a classmate. (2) Each of you draw 12 squares on a separate sheet of paper (like the ones on this page but larger). (3) Write a vocabulary word from one of your subjects in the top half of each rectangle. (You should each write the same words.) (4) Find and write the definition below each word. (5) Cut the rectangles apart. (6) Combine your cards with your partner's cards. (This will give you doubles of each word.) (7) Turn all cards facedown so the words don't show. (8) Play *Concentration*. Find the matching card for each word. *But*, each time you turn over a card, pronounce the word and read the definition. (9) When you make a match, remove the cards. Give yourself a point for each match.

problematic difficult to solve or decide: puzzling		

FOLLOW-UP • Play *Concentration* until you feel confident that you know all the words and their meanings.

USING FLASH CARDS

START-UP • Another useful strategy for learning and remembering just about anything is the *flash card*. Flash cards work especially well for learning new words. Try using this strategy in the activity below.

"I remember a quick flash!"

▶ Choose two to four words you don't know from your current reading (or from the dictionary). Write the words in rectangles, like the samples below. Cut the rectangles apart and place your words in a pile in the center of your desk or table. (Your partner or group members should do the same.) Working alone or in pairs, find the correct definition for each word and write it on the back of each vocab-card. Study these vocabulary words using one or more of the following strategies:

1. Use the vocab-cards like flash cards. One person holds up a word. The first person to give the correct definition receives that card.
2. One person reads a definition; the others write the vocabulary word for that definition. Arrange the vocab-cards in the order they were read so you can check your papers quickly.
3. Place all vocab-cards in a pile or small bag. Each person draws out a card and reads one side; the person then answers with either the matching vocabulary word or the definition. (This answer depends upon which side of the card was read.)

TIP Make and use flash cards often in all your classes. Foreign and technical words—especially those used in science and math—can be learned and remembered more easily by using flash cards.

FOLLOW-UP • Create a set of flash cards for something you are studying right now. Choose a topic or list you are expected to remember for a long time.

PART IV
Writing and Learning Minilessons

Covering the important areas

of writing, language, and learning

included in *Write Source 2000*

WRITING AND LEARNING MINILESSONS

Learning in Capsule Form

Let's say you've been working on a short story in language arts. Last night you thought of a great ending, and you can't wait to get your thoughts on paper as soon as class starts. But wait! Your teacher says she wants to start out today's class with a discussion on word choice. You immediately think to yourself, I don't have time for a discussion! I've got to get to my story! Then your teacher adds, "Don't worry. You will have plenty of time to work on your writing. This is only a minilesson."

That's the nice thing about minilessons. They don't take up a lot of time. They present learning material in capsule form—usually in 10- or 15-minute segments. And they leave plenty of class time for more important things—like writing stories.

The **Minilessons** in your SourceBook cover a number of important points related to writing and learning. For example, in one minilesson, you'll learn how to select a writing subject. In another minilesson, you'll learn how to correct comma splices. We offer a minilesson for nearly every important idea in your handbook. Read through your "User's Checklist" and see for yourself. Also read through some of the minilessons themselves. You've never seen learning like this before.

User's Checklist

Check your progress as you work on these **Minilessons.**

❑ **Selecting a Writing Subject** • *Alphabet Cluster*

❑ **Ideas for Short Stories** • *Butcher, Baker, Candlestick Maker*

❑ **Selecting a Writing Topic** • *Question Maker*

❑ **Avoiding Comma Splices** • *Comma Comma Down*

❑ **Identifying Comma Splices** • *Stand up for commas.*

❑ **Using Quotes Within Quotes** • *Thirdhand Words*

❑ **Exercises in Style** • *Sharpened Ax Today*

❑ **Writing a Character Sketch** • *Eyes Like Meteors*

- ❏ **Writing a Business Letter** • *Dear Mr. Zzyzz:*
- ❏ **Imitating a Poem** • *Whose Pants These Are*
- ❏ **Citing Borrowed Works** • *Credit Where Credit Is Due*
- ❏ **Using the Dictionary** • *Homographs*
- ❏ **Synthesizing Information** • *Get Down*
- ❏ **Improving Reading** • *Dear Sis,*
- ❏ **Improving Vocabulary** • *Polysyllables*
- ❏ **Using Context Clues** • *Hint! Hint!*
- ❏ **Improving Group Skills** • *Everybody, be quiet!*
- ❏ **Using an Ellipsis** • *The Gist of It*
- ❏ **Commas in a Series** • *Cold Serial*
- ❏ **Using Commas** • *Groundhogs*
- ❏ **Appositive Phrases** • *Choco*
- ❏ **Commas with Appositives** • *Are you appositive?*
- ❏ **Nonrestrictive Phrases and Clauses** • *Soup to Nuts*
- ❏ **Conjunctive Adverbs** • *Hot Time in the Old Town*
- ❏ **Using Colons** • *Lower the flow.*
- ❏ **Numerals in Compound Modifiers** • *Life and Death*
- ❏ **Indirect Quotations** • *Just Asking*
- ❏ **Block Quotations** • *At Your Fingertips*
- ❏ **Punctuating Titles** • *The Readaholic*
- ❏ **Using Parentheses** • *Enchanted, I'm sure.*
- ❏ **Capitalization** • *Trade Names*
- ❏ **Spelling: Forming Plurals** • *Attention, shoppers!*

- ❏ **Spelling** • *Bad Spellers' Dictionary*
- ❏ **Using the Right Word** • *Double Trouble*
- ❏ **Usage** • *The Right to Write*
- ❏ **Usage** • *I said "steel," not "steal."*
- ❏ **Simple Sentence Patterns** • *SVIODO*
- ❏ **Identifying Clauses** • *For a Good Clause*
- ❏ **Types of Sentences** • *What's in a name?*
- ❏ **Types of Sentences** • *That's Simple*
- ❏ **Intransitive Verbs** • *"To Be" or Not "To Be"*
- ❏ **Verb Tenses** • *Munchies*
- ❏ **Principal Parts of Irregular Verbs** • *All the Right Parts*
- ❏ **Transitive Verbs; Direct and Indirect Objects** • *Weird Objects*
- ❏ **Verbals** • *Let's play PIG!*
- ❏ **Verbals** • *Growing Sentences from Seed*
- ❏ **Adverbs** • *Adverb Ping-Pong Volley*
- ❏ **Using Word Parts** • *The Root of the Problem*
- ❏ **Understanding Conflict** • *That's a problem!*
- ❏ **Using Diagrams** • *The Working Parts*
- ❏ **Using Historical Documents** • *News from the Capital*
- ❏ **Using Historical Documents** • *They really said that?*
- ❏ **Using the Historical Time Line** • *Top Ten*

FOLLOW-UP • Write minilessons of your own about writing or language learning to share with members of your writing group or your entire class.

MINILESSONS

Alphabet Cluster . . . . *Selecting a Writing Subject*

A ▶ Read the directions for "Clustering" under "Selecting a Writing Subject" (**035**).

ASK your nearest neighbor to pick any letter of the alphabet.
WRITE DOWN a word that comes to mind starting with that letter.
USE that word as the "nucleus word" for a cluster.
DEVELOP your cluster until you run out of ideas.
PICK an idea from your cluster and
WRITE about it for 5 minutes.

Butcher, Baker, Candlestick Maker . . . . *Ideas for Short Stories*

B ▶ Read the humorous and insightful interview with the story writer Bob Kann (**239**). Then look over the "Essentials of Life Checklist" (**036**).

CHOOSE one "essential of life" from each of the three columns.
MAKE UP three characters, each one associated with one of your three "essentials of life."
BEGIN to write a story in which all three characters are forced to interact. WRITE the story to *find out* what they do.
WRITE fast and furiously for 5-8 minutes. Then MAKE NOTES to help you finish the story later.

Question Maker . . . . *Selecting a Writing Topic*

C ▶ Look at the "Essentials of Life Checklist" (**036**).

CREATE *five* different topics by repeating the following process five times: Pick one word from each of the three columns and make a good question out of it. For example:

| CLOTHING | MACHINES | RULES/LAWS |

- "What laws apply to the machines that manufacture clothing?"

| SENSES | PLANTS | FUEL |

- "What does a log sound like when it burns?"

If any of the questions lead you to a better idea, WRITE about it.

Comma Comma Down ..... *Avoiding Comma Splices*

A When writers don't notice where complete sentences stop and start, they often commit a punctuation error called a "comma splice." FIND OUT what comma splices are and how to avoid them by reading **477, 484,** and **092,** in that order.

READ the paragraph below and COUNT all the commas in it: _____

A splice is a connection between two ropes, the threads of one rope are woven together with threads from the other, if a splice is strong, the connection will hold, if it is weak, it will break, sentences are like ropes, if you want to put two complete sentences together, you must use a strong connection, a comma by itself is not strong enough, you must come to a full stop with a period or semicolon, or you may use a comma plus a conjunction the way this sentence does.

Now CIRCLE only those commas that are comma splices needing to be corrected. (Some of the commas are correct as they stand.) If you have extra time, REVISE this paragraph and WRITE it over so that it is correct from start to finish.

Stand up for commas. ... *Identifying Comma Splices*

B Review the definition of a "comma splice" (**092**).

HAVE one person stand in front of your class or writing group and read the sentence below *very* slowly, word by word. IF and WHEN you come to a comma splice, STAND UP beside your chair and say, "Comma splice." If there is any difference of opinion, DISCUSS who is right.

• At the stoplight, our car, a dented, rusty brown station wagon, stopped next to a sleek, flaming red Ferrari, we were so embarrassed.

Thirdhand Words .... *Using Quotes Within Quotes*

C In **109,** you'll find this quotation from the novelist Kurt Vonnegut:
"I myself find that I trust my own writing most . . . when I sound
like a person from Indianapolis, which is what I am."
HOW would you punctuate a sentence in which you quoted a friend, who was in turn quoting Vonnegut?

Here's a start. In the first space, WRITE the name of your friend. COMPLETE the rest of the sentence making use of Vonnegut's exact words:

_____ said, "I respect Kurt Vonnegut's honesty when he writes,

_____

_____

FIND OUT how to punctuate a quote within a quote in **513 and 515.**

Sharpened Ax Today............ *Exercises in Style*

A Browse around in the sections on "Styling Sentences" (**109-111**).

IMAGINE you are somebody quite different from who you are: an astronaut, a Miss America candidate, a lumberjack, a cab driver, a dolphin trainer, etc.

WRITE one page of that person's daily diary in the style you imagine that person would have. MAKE the style clearly different from your own.

Eyes Like Meteors........ *Writing a Character Sketch*

 B Read through the sections on writing a "Character Sketch" (**159-165**).

CHOOSE the person whom you either like most or admire most in your life.
REMIND yourself of the important ideas about detailed, colorful language in sections **118-122**.
MAKE two headings: "Physical Characteristics" and "Personal Characteristics."
Under each heading, LIST the finest details you can observe or remember.
CONCLUDE by writing a sentence that tells your single, strongest impression of the person. Don't settle for vague, general language here.

Dear Mr. Zzyzz: .... *Writing a Business Letter*

C Study the instructions for writing a business letter (**203-214**). Memorize the format called "Semiblock" (**204**). Next, GO THROUGH the list of "Writing Topics" in section **040** and pick any topic that especially interests you.

Now, PICK any name at random from your city's telephone book. Finally,
WRITE a business letter in semiblock form asking the person you've picked if he or she has any special information about your topic.

Whose Pants These Are .... *Imitating a Poem*

 D Read and appreciate the poem "Stopping by Woods on a Snowy Evening" by Robert Frost (**229**). Pay attention to the line length, the rhyme scheme, the rhythm, the subject, the word choice, the mood, etc.

WRITE a "parody" (a playfully twisted imitation) of Frost's poem. First,
CHANGE the word "woods" in the first line to any other word that makes some kind of sense (pants, gloves, car, house, cheese, pen, etc.).
ALTER the rest of the first line so that it fits your new word but still sounds "sort of" like Frost.
FINISH the poem in the same way. Don't be afraid to let your new poem take off on its own if it "wants" to.

Credit Where Credit Is Due ... *Citing Borrowed Works*

A Study **281** and **283** to learn about adding a bibliography or works cited page in a report. Then WRITE a correct bibliographic entry for the following book.

Title: <u>Why Do Clocks Run Clockwise?</u> Author: David Feldman, Publisher: Harper & Row, City of Publication: New York, Copyright Date: 1987

Homographs.................. *Using the Dictionary*

B If you will carefully study the sample page of a dictionary at **304** and read the labels in the margins, you will be able to answer the following question with one word:

What is the first part of speech of the third homograph of "spat"?

Answer: _____

Important Note: You must study the sample page at **304** carefully, or the above question will probably read like a menu in a Martian restaurant.

Get Down .... *Synthesizing Information*

C The opposite of going hungry is having *plenty,* right?
LOOK in *Write Source 2000,* **326**, at the way the authors have synthesized their thoughts on "HUNGER" by creating a "Title-Down Paragraph."

USE a "Title-Down Paragraph" to draw together whatever knowledge and attitudes you have about North America's "PLENTY."
Important Note: Make sure you understand what you are doing when you "synthesize."

Dear Sis, ... *Improving Reading*

D Suppose your school has assigned you to work with a younger student who is having trouble reading and remembering.

STUDY the chapter on "Study-Reading Skills" (**361-370**).
MAKE UP a name for your student.
WRITE a personal letter (see **196-202**) in which you give your student the best advice you know of for improving his or her reading.